FINACE DIVA

Epsilon Money is a new age Wealth management Company focussed on strategic financial planning for life's pivotal moments, be it marriage, education, parenthood, or retirement. By aligning financial strategies with individual life goals, we empower clients to make informed decisions. Our tailored approach ensures proactive steps towards a stable and prosperous future. With personalized guidance from experienced wealth managers backed by a strong product proposition, we help clients navigate through diverse financial landscapes, fostering trust and transparency. At Epsilon Money, we're committed to walk alongside clients, providing comfort and support to pursue their dreams with confidence. As an organization we have a special focus on Middle class and affluent investors, SMEs and have ambitions to grow across the expanse of our country, especially in Tier II and Tier III Cities in a Phy-gital mode. Epsilon Money is AMFI registered Mutual Fund Distributor & IRDAI Registered Corporate Agent.

Disclaimer

We are grateful to our colleagues and all those
who have provided invaluable support in the creation
of this book.

the Finance Diva

BY EPSILON MONEY

The legacy of Maa Lakshmi lives on in every woman, as a Finance Diva in her own right.

Mahati Pandya, Abhishek Dev

MEET
THE AUTHORS

Abhishek Dev
Co-Founder & CEO, Epsilon Money

Abhishek, a proven leader and passionate investment professional, has spent over 23 years in pursuit of excellence in Asset and Wealth Management Industry across India and ASEAN. His career trajectory, spanning esteemed Indian and Global Asset & Wealth Managers across various roles including Board Membership, Business Development, Strategy, Investment Advisory, Product Development etc, has provided him with 360-degree insights of various aspects in Wealth Management. This deep-seated passion for Wealth management and commitment to the cause of spreading financial literacy motivated him to establish the Epsilon Money Group in 2022 with a focus on Affluent, Middle class and SME Customers in Tier II & III cities. Abhishek strongly believes in empowering individuals, particularly women, to navigate financial landscapes with confidence which has led the group to establish an Investment Initiative focussed on Women under @ TM "The Finance Diva" initiative.

Mahati Pandya
AVP - Marketing & Strategy, Epsilon Money

Mahati exemplifies a strategic mind with a financial heart. While her expertise lies in marketing and business strategy, her passion for finance fuels her mission to empower women. Alongside Abhishek, she leads the impactful "Finance Diva" initiative, a testament to her dedication to financial education and inclusion for women. This initiative goes beyond just her professional pursuits, highlighting her drive to create positive change for women in the financial landscape. While she thrives in the dynamic world of business & marketing and embraces the opportunities it presents, she also finds joy in exploring art, literature, and the beauty of nature. This well-rounded perspective allows her to approach challenges with both creativity and a grounded perspective.

WELCOME MESSAGE

Laxmipat Dudheria
Co-Founder & Mentor, Epsilon Money Group

Wealth Creation, is both, an art and a science. It requires knowledge and hard work but even more, it requires discipline.

In our world, Women naturally epitomize these qualities. There is a reason why God chose women to bear children, give birth and take the cycle of life forward. Such responsibilities can only be borne with the greatest sense of responsibility.

Efficient management of household wealth or a firm's finances require similar discipline and sense of responsibility. The women of today are managing the wealth of our nation. We live in the era where our President, the Finance Minister and the financial markets regulator – SEBI's chairman are women.

In this era of Bharat's amritkal, we need to take this revolution in every home. Woman empowerment is incomplete without financial empowerment. This book, the first in "The Finance Diva Series" is our small and humble effort in encouraging women participation in financial decision making through inspiring examples which we all can relate to.

I hope you enjoy reading the book and spread the word.

INDEX

THE GENESIS

Pushing open the frosted glass door with a sigh, I stepped into Abhishek's office. His normally composed face was etched with a mixture of amusement and frustration. Abhishek, ever the picture of controlled chaos, swivelled in his ergonomic chair (it sometimes looks like the throne of thorns! to me), a half-eaten dark chocolate bar abandoned on the corner of his glass desk.

"...Looks like the market took a wilder ride than your lunch did, Abhishek. Rough morning?" I said as I walk into his cabin. "Mahati, come in, come in!" he exclaimed, gesturing towards the sleek black guest chair across from him. This guy is a passionate wealth manager who could decipher financial charts faster than you can say «bull market." Charts flickered on his screens; his phones always buzzed with market updates, the kinds whose only favourite channels are CNBC and Bloomberg!

"Did you hear what happened in Bangalore branch?" Abhishek began, a mischievous glint in his eye. "Our Regional Director in south spent an hour crafting a personalized investment plan for this CTO of an MNC, a high-powered woman – a self-made millionaire, no less!" I leaned in, "Nice! Did she invest?"

Abhishek chuckled, a wry note creeping into his voice. "Not exactly. After his hour-long presentation, detailing diversified portfolios and potential outcomes, the client leaned back and said, 'This sounds great and fits my requirements. But I'll have to run it by my husband and get his approval. Usually he is the one who understands and decides on financial matters". so we (Our RD and Her) have a meeting with her husband next week to convince him on the plan.

My jaw dropped. This wasn't uncommon, Abhishek explained. Despite being financially successful, many women still deferred financial decisions to their fathers / husbands. The reverse may also happen, but mostly it is women deferring their financial decision to men. It was a frustrating reality, a missed opportunity for women to take charge of their financial futures.

"There's a gap, Mahati," he said, his voice turning serious. "A gap between financial literacy and empowerment, especially for women. We need to help bridge it.»

"You know what I feel sometimes? March rolls around, and companies scramble for the "Woman of the Year" crown. Every March 8th, social media explodes with #WomenEmpowerment hashtags and campaigns. While celebrating women's achievements is fantastic, let's be honest: a one-day spotlight isn't enough. Pink campaigns and flowery discounts decorate the landscape, but most of them vanish in the thin air by April. Is woman a one-day campaign?" I say out with frustration.

This begs the question: Why are women, who form almost half the population and hold immense economic potential, underrepresented in financial planning conversations? Even when, study says Women tend to live longer than men, but often have less saved for retirement. Women aren't a monolithic group. They face a unique set of financial challenges throughout their lives, from the gender pay gap to the motherhood penalty. These issues require ongoing conversation and solutions, not just a fleeting trend.

I, fascinated by the intricacies of finance, found myself captivated by his stories about the human element – the anxieties, aspirations, and triumphs that danced around wealth management.

"Wouldn't it be amazing, Mahati," he mused, "to bridge the gap between financial literacy and storytelling? To create a narrative that not only entertains but empowers people to take control of their financial destinies? Wouldn't it be amazing if we could bridge the gap between finance and the everyday life of women? Most financial books are dry as toast, and frankly, intimidating! We need something relatable, something filled with stories that people can connect with."

Well, India's investment scene is like a crazy party – the economy's booming, everyone wants a piece of the pie, and the stock market is a wild ride. The problem? A huge chunk of the population, especially women, are still watching from the side-lines because they're scared they don't know enough. This isn't just about missing out on making money; it's about women taking control of their financial future and being a bigger part of India's economic success story.

His words struck a chord. As a woman navigating the complexities of money management myself, I knew exactly what he meant. The financial world often felt like a boys' club, shrouded in jargon and devoid of stories that resonated with the female experience.

That's how the idea for this initiative – The Finance Diva, was born. "Becoming a Finance Diva" the first book of this series Finance Diva, wouldn›t be a dry textbook, but a captivating story filled with relatable characters. We'd weave financial literacy into the narrative, letting our heroine learn the ropes alongside the reader. We wanted to dismantle the myth that finance was a daunting labyrinth and replace it with the exhilarating feeling of empowerment that comes with taking control of your financial destiny.

The seed was sown. We spent months brainstorming, our initial scribbles evolving into a concept that resonated deeply – a novel that would weave a captivating narrative with practical financial wisdom. Abhishek, his initial hesitation of being a male face behind this female-oriented initiative was replaced by a growing enthusiasm, unearthing stories from his experience, anonymized tales of successes and pitfalls that served as cautionary tales and testaments to resilience.

So, here we are, Abhishek and I, an unlikely team united by a shared passion – to show women that financial literacy is not just about numbers, but about building a life filled with freedom, security, and the occasional (or perhaps frequent!) retail therapy splurge.

This book isn't just a guide, it's an invitation. An invitation to join us on a journey of financial discovery, one where you'll learn the language of money, build confidence in your investment choices, and ultimately, become your own financial diva. Ready to rewrite the narrative? Let's begin!

BEYOND THE VELVET CHAIRS

FEMINISM
FIGHTS
FOR EQUAL
RIGHTS ,
NOT SPECIAL
FAVOURS.

SAMRUDDHI BANK
WEALTH , EMPOWERMENT , INDEPENDENCE
LAXMI SINGHANIA
CIO ,SAMRUDDHI BANK CHAIRMAN AND TRUSTEE SAHYOGINI TRUST
GIVE WOMEN
RIGHTS
OR WE WILL
FIGHT

I stood on the grand stage at the majestic Samruddhi Bank headquarters, in Nariman Point, Mumbai, and the spotlight was right on me. The collective click of cameras sounded like a symphony of curiosity. The room was packed with journalists, each seat occupied by an eager mind, a notebook, and an unspoken question.

They had assembled to seek my perspective on the freshly passed budget, a financial blueprint set to shape the economic destiny of our nation for the upcoming financial year. As the Chief Investment Officer at Samruddhi Bank, public speeches and press conferences were a routine part of my role. However, this particular day held a unique significance. The budget, a mysterious treasure chest of economic objectives and societal commitments, had sparked both enthusiasm and curiosity.

I was here not just as a finance expert, but as a guide through the intricate web of opportunities and challenges that lay ahead. This was especially important because this year's budget placed significant emphasis on women's welfare. One strong initiative, for instance, as the substantial increase in funding for women's entrepreneurship programs, aiming to empower women economically and foster financial independence.

On the grand screen behind me, an eye-catching header revealed the central theme of today's interview: "Laxmi's Vision: Wealth, Empowerment, Independence," accompanied by a photograph and my name – Laxmi

Singhania, CIO of Samruddhi Private Wealth Bank and Chairman & Trustee of Sahyogini Women's Trust. Oh, and let's not forget the delightful photograph they've chosen. I mean, who wouldn't adore a picture where I'm grinning so widely, with all my teeth on display and I look like a monkey? I've lost count of how many times I've begged my team not to use that image. I have a treasure trove of 100 better pictures, but here we are. I am sure I am screwing marketing team's happiness after this interview.

Yet, in a surprising turn of events, the theme resonated with me - deeply. Over the years, I had come to view finance as more than just a vessel for accumulating wealth; it was a means of nurturing prosperity with wisdom, using it to uplift society, and sowing the seeds of genuine abundance.

With a smile (hopefully not monkey-esque this time), I addressed the eager faces. I commenced, "Ladies and gentlemen, good afternoon. It's a privilege to be with you today to explore the profound implications of the recent budget on our financial landscape. Your presence and your inquiries underscore the importance of this fiscal journey. The budget is not just a financial plan; it's a narrative carved in the language of money.. Without further ado, I'd like to open the floor for questions."

The first question that came in was about my name, Laxmi, and its fancy connection to finances. The journalist, asked,

"So, Laxmi, your name is practically synonymous with the goddess of wealth. Any special financial superpowers you'd like to share?"

I couldn't help but grin, relishing the chance to dive into the symbolism behind my moniker. "You hit the nail on the head", my response echoed with gratitude as I remarked, "Thanks to my parents for giving me a name that's not just a label but a constant reminder of the values and principles I hold in the financial world!" I quipped. "Laxmi, the goddess of prosperity, is much revered in our culture. Her name isn't just about rolling in gold coins or materializing riches but also the virtues of wisdom, balance, and abundance. My role in finance is more than just numbers and investments. It encompasses wisdom in decision-making, balance in portfolio management, and a focus on the overall well-being of our clients. So, yeah, you could say I'm in the 'divine wealth management' business!" The journalists seemed intrigued by this analogy.

Another journalist raised a question that touched a chord with me. "Laxmi," she asked, "The investments and financial planning you discuss often appear tailored for modern, urban women. What about those in tier 2 cities and rural areas? How can they benefit from your expertise?"

I welcomed this opportunity to discuss the financial landscape beyond metropolitan cities. "This is a crucial issue to address," I affirmed. While it's true that my financial advice often wears a modern, urban attire, let's not forget that good money management transcends boundaries and demographics. Whether you're in the bustling heart of a metropolis like Bombay or in the quiet charm of a rural area, financial wisdom is universal. So, my tips and expertise aren't just for the city slickers; they're for everyone looking to make their money work smarter, not harder. Women, including those in rural areas, have been avid savers and responsible financial decision-makers since time immemorial. Allow me to share the story of Draupadi, a character from our ancient epic, the Mahabharata."

"Draupadi, a revered protagonist, her life story mirrors the diverse financial roles that women in India have historically played. She was not just a symbol of feminine grace, but also an embodiment of resourcefulness, wisdom, and astute financial management, then whether it is about managing finances on a limited budget or at the grand scale of governing a kingdom

During the Pandavas' exile, Draupadi's financial prowess shone as she astutely managed their limited resources. She ensured that the family's meager supplies of food, clothing, and essentials were used judiciously. Just like Draupadi, women have consistently demonstrated an innate knack for financial prudence. This unique trait empowers them to stretch available resources and make every rupee count, an invaluable skill passed down through generations. On the other hand, Draupadi's role as an advisor to Yudhishthira, the eldest Pandava, on financial and governance matters of the kingdom further underscores her financial wisdom. In India, women have often taken on advisory roles within their families and communities. They provide invaluable insights on financial decisions, investments, and the overall well-being of their households or organizations. Draupadi's ability to counsel Yudhishthira on matters of finance and governance reveals a deep understanding of ruling a kingdom. Her advisory brilliance aligns with the multifaceted financial roles that women have historically played in India. This is a powerful illustration of the inherent financial wisdom that Indian women possess. It reflects their ability to maximize every rupee's value, be it in budgeting for a family's needs or managing resources in a business. Just like Draupadi, women have consistently demonstrated an innate knack for financial prudence. Women have consistently contributed their financial wisdom to guide their families and communities towards financial prosperity and stability. Look at India's Finance Minister herself! In modern India, women have made significant strides in the financial world. They have excelled in various fields, including banking, finance, entrepreneurship, investments and making substantial contributions to the country's economic growth. Draupadi's legacy continues to inspire and reinforce the belief that women in India can and will play pivotal roles in shaping the financial landscape of the nation.".

I leaned forward in my plush velvet chair, the soft cushion embracing me like a trusted confidant. With a pause, I continued, " Forget sinking into velvet seats discussing finances – the real queens of budgeting are out there, hustling in tier 2 cities and rural havens. These women are financial ninjas, stretching every rupee, managing households like CEOs, and securing their families' futures better than any stockbroker. But guess what? They deserve more than just nods of appreciation. They deserve tools, knowledge, and access to modern financial avenues to truly unleash their financial power!

And the good news is, the government is listening! This year's budget sings a new tune, focusing on boosting rural income and empowering women, especially those in self-help groups (SHGs). SHGs have proven their value, especially during the challenges posed by the COVID-19 pandemic, and they are expected to contribute to expanding women's participation in the labour force. Now, the government's giving them a leg up with raw materials, marketing support, and the chance to become economic powerhouses. Imagine that – more women leading the charge, expanding their reach, and contributing to a stronger workforce!

One noteworthy announcement in the budget is the introduction of the Mahila Samman Saving Certificate, a one-time small savings scheme designed exclusively for women. This scheme offers a fixed interest rate of 7.5% and allows deposits of up to 2 lakhs in the name of women or girl children for a maximum two-year tenure. It also includes a partial withdrawal option for emergencies, making it a valuable financial resource for Indian women.

In conclusion, the recent Union Budget presents a compelling effort to strengthen the financial independence and economic empowerment of Indian women, particularly in tier 2 cities and rural areas. It recognizes the pivotal role they play in the nation's growth and development, setting the stage for a brighter and more inclusive financial future for India."

I emphasized the importance of financial education and access to suitable financial instruments, concluding with a testament to women's financial strength. " So, let's move beyond plush chairs and empower the real financial rockstars – the women who make every rupee count, no matter where they live. Their journey to financial freedom has just begun, and it's a story worth cheering for! Financial power knows no zip code, only empowered individuals ready to claim it!"

The room was filled with thoughtful nods and scribbling pens, and I knew that my message had resonated with the audience. In my previous PR sessions, the questions mainly revolved around market trends, investment opportunities, and budget impacts. I had confidently tackled those finance-related queries with my wealth of experience.

However, this time, the focus was different. The theme of "Laxmi's Vision" emphasized women's financial empowerment and its social impact. I felt a mix of nervousness and excitement in the air. Taking a deep breath, I announced a 15-minute break before we continued.

I stepped off the stage and found my PR Head Aman, who arranged me this session, with a big grin. He handed me a coffee. "I didn't see that coming," Aman said, taking a sip of coffee. "that was quite a twist in the interview today. Were you ready for all the attention on 'Laxmi's Vision'?"

"It's refreshing, though, to see this newfound interest. It's not every day you get to inspire change, right?" I chuckled.. "but next time, I might need a double shot of espresso to brace myself for these delightful surprises"

"Noted, Laxmi. I'll make sure we have extra espresso on standby." Winked Aman. We shared a laugh and, after taking one final sip of coffee, I made my way back to the stage. Journalists leaped up to fire further questions.

Amidst the polite inquiries, a voice rang out, sharp and laced with righteous anger. The air crackled with tension within me as I faced my unexpected guest in the audience - Meera Kohli, firebrand leader of the "Daughters of Shakti," a renowned feminist group known for their bold activism. Clashing prints on her flowing skirt and a bold slogan on her worn leather jacket announced Meera's fiery brand of feminism, a confident smirk framing fiery red lipstick, her kohl-rimmed eyes mirroring the challenge and hope in her gaze.

"Ms. Singhania," Meera began, her voice sharp with skepticism, "I wouldn't have sought this audience unless desperation had truly set in. Your 'Vision' of financial empowerment sounds promising, but let's be real," she paused, her tone laced with raw frustration, "the numbers speak for themselves."

"Many women across the board, doctors, teachers, even CEOs, still earn significantly less than their male counterparts, sometimes for doing the exact same job. So, tell me," she leaned forward, her gaze burning into mine, "if there's no equal pay between men and women, why should there be equal taxation?"

Silence stretched, the weight of her question heavy in the air. I knew her frustration mirrored the anger countless women felt. The gender pay gap was a gaping wound, and Meera's proposal, however radical, resonated with a primal desire for fairness.

I took a deep breath, choosing my words carefully. "I understand your anger, Meera. The pay gap is a stark reality, a stain on our society. But creating separate tax brackets for men and women, while seemingly appealing, could have unintended consequences."

"Why?" she challenged, her voice sharp. "Doesn't it directly address the income disparity? Women earn less, so they should pay less tax, right?"

"While the sentiment is noble," I responded, my tone patient, "it risks creating a system that reinforces the very inequality we're fighting. Firstly, it assumes a universal pay gap across all professions and income levels, which isn't the case. Secondly, it could discourage women from pursuing higher-paying careers, knowing they'd be taxed at a higher rate."

Meera scoffed. "Isn't that already happening? Women face systemic barriers even before choosing careers, then get penalized for choosing higher-paying fields just because they're expected to shoulder more domestic responsibilities."

I nodded in agreement. "Absolutely. That's why we need to fight for equal pay and dismantle the biases that hold women back. But separate tax brackets wouldn't solve those core issues. Instead, it could create a perception that women are inherently less capable of earning high incomes, which is simply untrue."

She narrowed her eyes, her voice now tinged with suspicion. "So, what then? We just accept this injustice?"

"Absolutely not!" I said with conviction. "We fight it on multiple fronts. Advocating for equal pay legislation, promoting policies that support working parents, and encouraging girls to pursue STEM fields are crucial steps. Additionally, we need to address the underlying societal norms that undervalue women's work and contributions."

"But that takes time," Meera argued, her frustration simmering. "Women need relief now."

"I understand your urgency, Meera," I said, my voice softening. "Believe me, I do. But quick fixes often have unintended consequences. Instead, let's push for solutions that address the root causes and create a truly equal paying field for all. Sustainable change might take time, but it's the only way to build a future where women are not just treated equally, but valued and empowered in every sphere."

A flicker of understanding softened Meera's gaze. "Empowered, not pitied," she muttered, more to herself than me.

"Exactly," I affirmed. "And that empowerment starts with recognizing the complexities of the issue and working together for solutions that benefit all women, not just through quick fixes that might create new problems."

A tense silence settled, then Meera offered a hesitant nod. "Perhaps you're right, Ms. Singhania. But know this," her voice regained its fiery edge, "the Daughters of Shakti won't rest until every woman receives the respect and opportunities she deserves."

"And," I smiled, extending a hand, "Samruddhi Bank stands with you in that fight. Let's not be adversaries, Meera, but allies in this battle for true equality."

As the Press Conference drew to a close, I couldn't help but feel a sense of optimism. The unexpected shift in the interview's focus toward women's financial empowerment had sparked lively discussions and unveiled a new realm of possibilities. With the audience's applause still ringing in my ears, I expressed my gratitude for their thoughtful questions and engaged participation.

The live screen behind me displaying the day's theme: "Laxmi's Vision: Wealth, Empowerment, Independence" was a fitting reminder that finance isn't just about wealth accumulation but also about nurturing wisdom and ensuring financial well-being for all, regardless of gender.

With that, I announced the conclusion of the session, promising more insights and revelations in the journey ahead. It was a moment of promise, a new chapter in the making, and the beginning of an exciting exploration of finance, empowerment, and my enduring spirit redefining women's financial independence through 'Laxmi's Vision'.

CHAPTER 02

THE PRICE OF PASSION

ARE YOU READY TO BE THE SUPERHERO OF OUR TOY BUDGET ADVENTURE?
MOM

The day was gradually fading, and I made my way back to my cabin, determined to tackle the remaining tasks of the day efficiently. Little did I know, an unexpected encounter awaited me, one that would challenge my understanding of the financial world.

Anyways, today, I had a special commitment waiting for me – taking my 5-year-old daughter, Ruhi, for toy shopping. She had been stubbornly persistent about this toy shopping since the last month, and I couldn't bear to keep her waiting any longer.

Earlier in the day, a successful press conference had left me feeling like a financial warrior returning from a victorious battle. But unlike weary warriors, the financial world never sleeps. There was always more to be accomplished, more lives to touch with the power of financial empowerment. As I glanced through my emails, one subject line grabbed my attention: "Business Loan Application – Rejection."

Curiosity piqued; I opened the e-mail. It was a loan application from a young woman, merely 25 years old, with significant aspirations. She had her sights set on opening her own fashion boutique, an entrepreneurial dream fuelled by her passion for design & innovation.

The loan application was a bold request for a sum of 2 crores, mirroring the audacity of her dreams. I noted her current occupation, as a Tech Associate at a reputable IT firm, pocketing a comfortable income Rs. 1,50,000 per month.

However, as I delved deeper into the email, the cruel word "Rejection" cast a shadow on her aspirations. Her application had been rejected due to reasons that seemed perplexing to me. The e-mail cited several criteria that the applicant did not meet, leaving me puzzled about the injustice of the financial world. I needed to understand more about this situation, and with determination, I picked up the phone and dialled the number of the senior relationship manager, Rajat Mehta, who had sent the email.

Rajat Mehta, a seasoned banking professional, was quick to respond. "Well, well well, Ms. Laxmi, I have a feeling I know exactly why you've reached out to me, but I must admit, I do appreciate the rare moments when you remember me…" joked Rajat. "So, Mr. Mehta, always straight to the point, I see. Would you be willing to spare 20 minutes of your precious time to discuss this case of Rhea Kapoor?" I chuckled, responding teasingly. "Coming", Rajat answered.

Rajat knocks the door, "May I come in madam, for the business date you just scheduled?" Rajat winks. "hmm…" I nodded, "Get straight into Rhea Kapoor's case".

"Laxmi," he began, "I'm glad you reached out about this case. I wanted to brief you on the details and reasoning behind the rejection. The applicant, Ms. Rhea Kapoor, is undoubtedly an enthusiastic and promising individual. She has a Demat Account with us since last 3 years and her investment journey with us started with systematic investment plans (SIPs) and do-it-yourself (DIY) stock investments, showcasing an early penchant for finance. And now she aims higher than her humble beginnings, dreaming of opening her own fashion boutique. It was a reflection of her deep passion for design and her entrepreneurial spirit. Her dream wasn't just about opening a fashion boutique; it was about revolutionizing clothing purchases, weaving sustainability and technology into a seamless experience. Rhea developed a groundbreaking app – a digital haven for eco-conscious shoppers. Unlike other platforms, her app didn't rely on models with perfect proportions, but on the magic of AI. This AI technology could virtually "fit" clothes on you, eliminating the guesswork and frustration of online shopping. We had personally witnessed the app, and its potential was undeniable."

I listened intently, eager for Rajat to comprehend the situation fully. Rajat continued, "However, when we evaluate loan applications, we follow certain financial criteria to mitigate risks. The primary concern here is that Ms. Kapoor's monthly income from her current job is Rs. 1,50,000. This falls way below the minimum income threshold required to support an unsecured loan of 2 Crores. Furthermore, her young age and limited professional experience make her a higher-risk candidate. The stringent criteria we employ to assess applicants necessitate that an individual must have a certain level of financial stability and experience before undertaking such a significant loan."

I contemplated the situation, recognizing the need for rigorous standards to safeguard financial stability. However, my thoughts kept returning to the young woman who stood at the precipice of her dream. There had to be a way to bridge the gap between her aspirations and the realities of financial eligibility.

"Rajat, I'll also enlighten you about rather more intriguing case. We recently received a business loan application, rather a substantial one, for 10 crores. The applicant, to put it mildly, appeared somewhat incompetent in handling such a significant sum for his business venture."

Rajat's curiosity piqued, and I saw him lean in, asking, "So, what's the catch?"

My voice took on a tone of frustration and disappointment as I continued, "The catch is that this applicant's father is a prominent figure, a real big shot, and a long-standing privileged customer of our bank. The family has a history of maintaining substantial deposits and investments with us, which they've done faithfully for years, and of course some of it has been pledged to support this loan."

Rajat furrowed his brows, starting to understand the dilemma. "So, the bank approved the loan application because of the father's influence and their long-standing relationship, even though the applicant himself didn't seem qualified?"

I nodded; my words heavy with the ethical predicament we faced. "Exactly, but they had put up a collateral. The bank approved the loan all because of the father's clout and the prospect of maintaining a valuable client. But in doing so, we're doing a great disservice to the dreams and potential of applicants like the Rhea Kapoor who got rejected for a much smaller loan, though I understand she meets limited criteria, but as you mentioned she seems competent enough".

I read a this somewhere which is perfectly resonating with a situation right now - "हुनर" सड़कों पर तमाशा करता है और "किस्मत" महलों में राज करती है!

''Rajat," I continued "Our bank follows one principle which we need to collectively follow – empower dreams and make the seemingly impossible, possible. Why don't you fix me a meeting with Rhea tomorrow I want to take a comprehensive understanding of her business plans, the specific niche or segment she aims to target in the fashion industry, her unique value proposition, and her long-term goals. This meeting will serve as a platform to explore the potential synergies between her vision and our financial support. I'm aware that bank won't be giving any financial assistance to her, but I am keen on understanding her business model thoroughly and ascertain the scope of her venture. I would appreciate it if you could share the meeting schedule via e-mail and send me a detailed report on her investments and CIBIL score."

Rajat promised to arrange the meeting for tomorrow and left. I glanced at the wall clock in my office. It read 6:30 PM, and my mind swiftly shifted to the special commitment I had been looking forward to all day. I rushed out of my office, juggling my bags and files, making a mental checklist of the things I needed to finish up tomorrow.

One of my colleagues couldn't resist passing a witty pun, "Arey Laxmi, aaj half day?" The gentle teasing brought a hearty laugh to me. It was indeed a rare occasion that I got to leave the office early, unlike today.

I made my way to the parking lot and called my driver. As he drove me through the bustling busy streets of Mumbai, I could see him frowning at the jammed traffic of evening peak hours. My phone rang, and I noticed it was Ruhi's nanny calling. Answering the call, I was greeted by Ruhi's enthusiastic voice – Hey Mommmyyyy!

"Hi, sweetie!" I chimed, trying to keep the enthusiasm in my voice.

"Mommy, you're finally coming! You promised today is our toy shopping day!" Ruhi's excitement was evident in every word.

"Yes, my love, I remember. I just finished some work, and now I'm on my way to pick you up. Are you all set for our adventure?"

She exclaims, "Yes, Mommy! I want a big fluffy teddy bear, a sparkly princess dress, a tiara, magic wand, and a spiderman action figure."

She began listing her desired toys, and it was clear she had put a lot of thought into it.

"Those sound like fantastic toys, Ruhi! But here's a fun idea. I'll come home and tell you. Wait for me, ok?"

I got home after a long and tiring drive through Mumbai's busy evening traffic. It took around an hour, even though it's just a 20-minute drive from office to home which is from Nariman Point to Lower Parel. Ruhi came to me bouncing with anticipation as soon as a stepped into the house.

"Ready, Mom?" she asked, her eyes wide with excitement.

"Give me just two minutes, honey. Let me change into something more comfortable," I replied, ruffling her hair and making a mental note to teach her some patience.

I retreated to the kitchen to grab a quick breather and a sip of my favourite rose-mint tea. There's something about the soothing aroma and delicate flavour that helps me recharge, even in the midst of evening routine.

I heard an unexpected voice from the kitchen. It was my brother. Ruhi had apparently pulled off a surprise that even I wasn't prepared for.

Ruhi, with her unmistakable enthusiasm, appeared behind me. "Mom, I invited Mama to join us for toy shopping!"

My brother, Vatsal, stood there with a spoon in his hand, taking a bite of the cake I had attempted to bake earlier in the morning. He couldn't resist making a sarcastic comment, "Is this a cake or a charcoal brick?"

I replied, "Let's not revisit that, Vatsal. I'm sticking to ordering cakes from now on."

Vatsal, with a mischievous grin, teased, "You know, you could've been a famous chef with your signature dish, 'The Carbon Cake.'"

I played along, saying, "Oh, absolutely. I'll take that secret recipe to my grave! You know, it took me two hours to bake this and once I was done, the kitchen looked like a war zone."

I grabbed a notebook and crayons from Ruhi's toy cabinet and sat down with her, "Chalo Ruhi, let's make a plan for your toys, and we decide how much money we can spend on each one."

Teaching Ruhi the importance of budgeting at a young age was vital to instill responsible financial habits early on. While the world of toys and shopping seemed like a delightful playground to her, it was an opportunity for me to introduce her to the concepts of budgeting, prioritizing, and making informed choices. By helping her to set a budget for her toy shopping, I aimed to teach her the value of money, making her understand that every rupee spent should be a thoughtful decision. It was a small step towards building a strong foundation of financial literacy that would serve her well in the future.

I explained, "We can decide how much money we want to spend on toys in total today and then divide that amount among the toys on your list. This way, you'll know how much you can spend on each toy, and we won't go over our budget.

Let's make our toy shopping adventure even more exciting. Imagine we have a magical budget to spend on the toys you want, which are – A Teddy Bear, a sparkling dress, tiara, magical wand and spiderman"

I help Ruhi list down all the toys in her notebook and create a table to set aside the right amount of money for each toy. "How about we decide on a budget of 10,000 rupees for today? You can spend this money on your desired toys. It's important to stick to the budget so we can save some money for other fun things in the future, or maybe a pizza treat this Sunday? OK?"

"OK" Ruhi exclaims. I could see some curiosity on her face.

"We'll start with 2000 rupees for a big, cuddly teddy bear, 3000 rupees for the sparkliest princess dress you've ever seen, 1000 rupees for a shiny tiara, 500 rupees for a magical wand, and 2500 rupees for a brave Spiderman action figure. But wait, we're not done! We'll also set aside 1000 rupees for cool puzzles to challenge your super-smart brain.

Now, here's the fun part, Ruhi. We have our budget, and as we pick our toys, Mumma will help you to subtract the money we spend from our budget. It's like a magical adventure where we learn to make choices and count money while having a blast! So, are you ready to be the superhero of our toy budget adventure?"

Her understanding and willingness to learn about budgeting warmed my heart. It was a small step, but an essential one in teaching her the value of money and responsible spending. Our toy shopping adventure was not just about fulfilling her wishes; it was a valuable lesson in financial responsibility and the joy of making thoughtful choices.

"Ruhi, we will go to some other toy store for shopping today! We won't go to Charlie's this time"

Vatsal raises an eyebrow, "Oh, Laxmi, what's wrong with Charlie's? Ruhi loves that place, and it's like a kiddie paradise."

I smirked, "Well, last time when we went to Charlie's, Ruhi had her heart set on buying every toy in the store. It seems they have some pretty effective sales tactics over there.

The very first time we visited Charlie's, they had a special event going on. They had people dressed up as larger-than-life cartoon characters, walking around and interacting with the children. Ruhi absolutely loved it, and they were incredibly kind to her, treating her like a little princess. After that experience, she's been a Charlie's fan for life. Most of the toys she's interested in at Charlie's tend to be on the pricier side, starting at around 5000 to 6000 rupees"

"Come on, sis, those expensive toys are like investments in her future. They're made with unicorn tears, and they sparkle with stardust", Vatsal grinned.

"Hein? Unicorn tears? The only tears I see are the ones shed by my wallet when I'm at the cash counter."

"Come on, Laxmi, they're expensive because they're non-toxic, safe for kids" Vatsal flashed a warm smile and gently patted Ruhi's head. I rolled my eyes, "Non-toxic, eh? Well, you used to eat mud, crayons, bricks, and lick walls when you were a kid, and you turned out fine." We laugh together as Vatsal continues, "Touche! Those mudpies were gourmet!"

"Alright, alright, we'll find some non-toxic, budget-friendly toys this time. Ruhi doesn't need a college fund just for her toys".

I grab my car keys and we head out for our toy shopping trip.

As we explored the store, Ruhi kept an eye on the price tags, making sure she stayed within her budget. She'd pick up a toy, look at the price, and then check her notepad to see if it fits her plan. If it did, she'd put it in the cart with a satisfied smile. If it didn't, she'd make a thoughtful decision to put it back on the shelf, knowing that she had other toys to buy.

In today's dynamic world, financial literacy is no longer a luxury, but an essential life skill. While formal education often comes later, the seeds of financial responsibility can be sown as early as the toddler years. Here's why equipping your little one with "piggy bank power" is an investment in their future. While it's never too early to start learning about money, instilling budgeting and savings skills in small children lays the groundwork for a lifetime of responsible financial habits. Budgeting is a fundamental aspect of financial literacy, and the earlier children grasp these concepts, the better equipped they are to navigate the complexities of managing money.

By assigning allowances or helping them manage small amounts of money, children learn the consequences of their spending choices. These early lessons contribute to the development of responsible habits, emphasizing the importance of saving, setting goals, and making thoughtful purchasing decisions. Budgeting also encourages children to prioritize their needs over wants. By understanding that resources are finite, children learn to allocate their funds wisely. This skill is invaluable in fostering a mindset that distinguishes between essential expenses and discretionary spending, promoting financial responsibility and discipline. By introducing children to the concept of saving within a budget, they develop the habit of putting money aside for specific purposes.

While formal financial education typically comes later, a child's financial literacy journey begins much earlier - in the heart of their family. Through everyday interactions and observations, toddlers begin to grasp fundamental financial concepts, even if they don't explicitly understand the terminology. By observing and mimicking family's financial behaviors, children begin to develop their own financial understanding and lay the foundation for responsible financial choices in the future.

Therefore, it's crucial for parents and caregivers to be mindful of their own financial behaviors and language around their children. These seemingly ordinary interactions hold the power to shape a child's financial journey in profound ways.

CHAPTER 3
RISK ROULETTE

IMAGINE, YOU'RE AT A CASINO, MESMERIZED BY THE ROULETTE WHEEL. YOU PLACE YOUR ENTIRE WAD OF CASH ON RED, CONVINCED IT'S A SURE THING. BUT AS THE BALL LANDS ON BLACK, YOUR DREAM OF RICHES VANISH FASTER THAN A MAGICIAN'S RABBIT. THAT, MY FRIEND, IS THE DANGER OF PUTTING ALL YOUR EGGS IN ONE BASKET.
"OUR AIM IS FINANCIAL FREEDOM."
EQUITY
DEBT
ALTERNATE

The next morning, I make my way into the office, leisurely walking down the corridor toward our fully glass-encased workspace. The sun had just begun to cast its warm, golden rays, and I could sense the promise of a day brimming with fresh new opportunities for the day.

Before entering my cabin, I bumped into Rajat. "Good morning, Rajat," I greeted him. "Good morning, Laxmi," Rajat replied, a smile gracing his face. "Please mail me the detailed reports on Rhea Kapoor's investments in SIPs and stocks, as well as her credit score" I requested.

"Indeed, Laxmi, I've sent those detailed reports to your email, just 2 mins ago," Rajat informed me.

"Excellent, thank you. And could we get a meeting with her as discussed? " I inquired further.

Rajat nodded, "Yes, Laxmi, the meeting is scheduled for 4 pm. I checked your calendar, it was free."

"Perfect, thank you for your promptness, Rajat." I said, appreciating his diligence and went to my cabin.

I pulled the blinds open in my cabin, revealing a stunning view of the ocean. The waves, gently kissing the shore, had always been a source of comfort, much like a father to me.

As I stood there, gazing at the endless ocean everyday, I couldn't help but feel an unspoken connection with the ocean. It often conveyed to me that life, just like the sea, was in a constant state of flux. Success, it whispered, belonged to those who learned to navigate and adapt to its ever-shifting tides. This daily ritual of observing the ocean through my workspace allowed me to start each day with a profound sense of purpose and a deep understanding of the boundless possibilities that the world held. It was during these moments, beside these serene waters, that I often found the clarity I needed to untangle life's most complex challenges. Hence, I've always said, the sea has been my father.

I moved to my desk, a sleek, glass-topped surface that offered a view of the ocean while I worked. With a sense of purpose, I began jotting down my tasks for the day and began going through my e-Mails. In the midst of a flood of ten-thousand emails, my eyes caught a glimpse of Rhea Kapoor's comprehensive investment report, sent by Rajat. Her investment journey with Samruddhi Bank in the last 3 years began with a strong commitment, as she initiated a SIP (Systematic Investment Plan) of ₹25,000 per month in the first year, designed for a 10-year investment tenure. This SIP allocation included ₹15,000 towards a diversified Equity Mutual Fund and ₹10,000 for a Debt Mutual Fund.

The following year, she expanded her investment strategy by initiating another ₹10,000 SIP, this time directed towards an Aggressive Hybrid Fund with a 9-year tenure. In the third year, Rhea further diversified her investments. She introduced a ₹2,000 monthly SIP in an Equity-

Linked Savings Scheme (ELSS) and allocated ₹4,000 per month for a Unit-Linked Insurance Plan (ULIP).

In addition to her mutual fund investments, Rhea has consistently allocated ₹10,000 to ₹12,000 each month into various stocks over the past three years. Her investment approach showcases a blend of both structured, long-term SIPs and stock market participation, reflecting a balanced strategy with the potential for growth and wealth accumulation. Now, turning our attention to observations, we can discern several significant insights from Rhea's investments in both Mutual Funds and the stock market. In her Mutual Funds' investments, the following points come to light:

Total Amount Invested till now – ₹12,12,000
Current Value – ₹14,66,054

Diversified Approach: Rhea adopts a diversified approach to her SIP investments. She has divided her monthly investments into Equity Mutual Funds, Debt Mutual Funds, Aggressive Hybrid Funds, ELSS, ULIPs, and individual stocks. This diversification can potentially reduce risk and improve returns.

Long-Term Focus: Rhea's choice of a 10-year tenure for her initial SIP in Equity Mutual Funds reflects a long-term investment outlook. Long-term investments can harness the power of compounding and provide substantial returns over time.

Progressive Investment Strategy: Over the years, Rhea has systematically expanded her investment portfolio. She started with two SIPs and then added ELSS and ULIPs.

Balanced Risk and Return: By investing in both mutual funds and individual stocks, Rhea has achieved a balance between potential risks and returns. Mutual funds offer diversification, while individual stocks provide opportunities for higher returns.

Tax Planning: Rhea's choice of ELSS, which qualifies for tax deductions under Section 80C, shows a prudent approach to tax planning. It not only helps in saving taxes but also serves as an avenue for long-term wealth creation.

Consistency & Discipline: One of the most notable aspects of Rhea's investment strategy is her consistent monthly investments in various avenues. This discipline is a critical factor in accumulating wealth and achieving financial goals.

Opportunity for Growth: The presence of an Aggressive Hybrid Fund in her portfolio suggests a willingness to take on a slightly higher risk for the potential of greater returns. This aligns with her long-term investment horizon.

Now coming to her stock investments, the following points come to light:

Total Amount Invested till now – ₹4,21,770
Current Value – ₹4,76,600

In analysing Rhea Kapoor's stock market investments, we observe that while her systematic investment plans (SIPs) have generated commendable returns, her stock investments exhibit certain characteristics. It's essential to recognize that when it comes to stock investments, a combination of "time in the market" and "timing the market" can significantly impact overall returns.

In the context of her stock investments, Rhea's disciplined approach in her SIPs contrasts with her stock portfolio strategy. During the three-year period, there were opportunities for her to potentially earn substantial returns if she had considered both factors, *time in the market*' and '*reasonable valuation.*'

The Importance of "Time in the Market":

"Time in the market" refers to the long-term approach of staying invested and letting your investments grow over an extended period. It's a crucial aspect of investing because it allows you to benefit from the compounding effect, where your returns generate additional returns over time. Rhea Kapoor's disciplined approach to SIPs demonstrates the power of staying invested in diversified equity and debt mutual funds. By patiently contributing to these SIPs over a more extended period (10 years for equity and 15 years for debt), she's likely to enjoy the benefits of compounding and rupee-cost averaging. This approach provides stability and a higher probability of consistent returns, thereby reducing the impact of market volatility.

Ideally, with a more selective and informed approach, she could have harnessed an estimated 87% index returns over the same three-year period, after looking her choice of stocks. The discrepancy between the estimated and actual returns emphasizes the importance of timing the market. Making well-informed choices about when to buy and sell stocks can lead to superior returns. Proper timing can help investors take advantage of market upswings, maximize gains, and minimize losses.

Balancing Both Approaches:

Rhea's investment journey showcases the significance of a balanced approach that combines disciplined, long-term strategies with informed stock market investments. While staying invested over time is crucial for building wealth steadily, her stock portfolio's performance highlights the need to consider market conditions and trends. By incorporating a well-researched, methodical approach to stock investing, individuals can harness the full potential of their investments.

In conclusion, the stock market is dynamic and volatile. Market trends change in a short span of time, even daily, and thus if you are seeing prices going up in the morning hours for a stock, it might become sluggish as the trading session is about to end. The stock market is volatile as it depends on multiple factors such as geopolitical issues, economic conditions, socio-economic situations, fundamental factors of the companies, and even on climatic conditions. Yes, if there is a below-average monsoon in a year, the stock market gets sluggish, as agriculture is a huge part of our economy.

So, to time the market, you need to be aware not only of all these factors but also myriad others since a small policy change in some part of the world can trigger a rally or a collapse in our markets. It is not possible to predict each of them so that you can put yours into the right stock at the right time. Do you think that is possible, timing the market every time and earning profits out of it? Practically, it is impossible, and you cannot predict weather conditions, war, or situations like Covid-19.

However, sadly enough, most people wait for the right time to enter or exit the market. While for traders, timing the market is essential as they buy and sell daily, timing the market doesn't have much impact when you think about long-term investment success. This brings us to a disciplined investment approach.

As the reminder for my next calendar appointment popped up on my screen, I realized it was time for our scheduled meeting with Mr. Rajesh, one of our investors. He had entrusted an investment advisory service for a substantial portfolio of 32 crores to our management.

The clock struck 12 noon, and just as the hands aligned perfectly, Mr. Rajesh, an imposing figure with a history of chaotic investments, walked into my cabin along with his wife - Rajni. After carefully understanding his risk profile, our recommendations always emphasized a balanced portfolio, with no more than 65% allocated to equities. However, driven by an insatiable appetite for higher returns, Rajesh had disregarded our advice and ventured into the risky territory of 85-90% equity allocation.

As he stormed into my office, visibly agitated, I knew it wasn't a routine meeting. His portfolio had taken a hit, not only in terms of returns but also its capital value. Rajesh's face was a storm of frustration as he exclaimed, "Laxmi, this is a very costly mistake! I invested in all the asset classes exactly as you suggested, using the same funds. How can I be at a loss?" He appeared to be at a loss, realizing the consequences of his choices.

Asset Type/class	Asset Allocation (Model%)	Actual Allocation % (by Rajesh)
Equity	**60%**	**89%**
Large Cap Fund	38%	20%
Small Cap Fund	10%	30%
Mid Cap Fund	12%	39%
Debt	**30%**	**11%**
Short Term Debt Fund / NCD	15%	6%
Corporate Fixed Deposit	15%	5%

Alternatives	10%	-
REITs	5%	-
Gold	5%	-
Total	**100%**	**100%**

I pulled up a report on my screen, and a quick glance revealed the glaring issue. Our carefully crafted asset allocation, which was designed to align with his risk profile, showed that nearly 65% of his investments were allocated to equities. It was clear that he had significantly deviated from the well-thought-out strategy we had proposed from 65% to staggering 89% in equities, and even there higher than suggested into riskier small and mid caps.

Taking a deep breath, I began to explain, " I understand that you followed the asset classes and funds, but what about asset allocation? This wasn't what we suggested. Mr. Rajesh, our primary focus at Samruddhi Bank is to safeguard our clients' capital. We strive to ensure that their investments not only generate returns but also preserve the wealth they have worked hard to accumulate. This is why we insist on maintaining a balanced and conservative approach to asset allocation."

I continued, "By carefully studying your risk profile, we had recommended a well-diversified allocation that included equities, fixed income, and other asset classes. However, with a significant portion of your portfolio in equities, you've exposed yourself to unnecessary risk.

While equities offer the potential for higher returns, they also come with a higher level of volatility. Additionally, within your equities allocation, there is significant exposure to small-cap, which may require research time and lot of expertise. Our approach is to carefully balance risk and reward, ensuring that your investments align with your financial goals and risk tolerance."

I went on to emphasize, "Our main objective is to be prudent and responsible stewards of your capital. This means that we strive to provide you with top-notch asset allocation, ensuring that your investments are aligned with your risk profile, investment horizon, and financial objectives."

Rajesh's frustration began to wane as he realized the importance of a well-considered asset allocation strategy. It was a costly lesson, but one that underscored the value of our conservative approach in wealth management.

Rajesh leaned back in his chair and sighed, "Laxmi, I honestly have a massive business to handle. I tend to overlook these finer details. From now on, my wife Rajni will oversee all these investments. That's why she's here with us for the meeting today."

Turning to Rajni with interest, I ask, 'So Rajni, first of all, nice meeting you. Could you tell me about your professional pursuits?" Rajni replies, "Oh, no, no. I take care of my home and family; I'm a homemaker." As soon as Rajni says 'Homemaker', Rajesh immediately interrupts, "She has chosen the noble role of making our house a home. In her hands, our home transforms into a place of comfort and joy."

Seeing Rajni join Mr. Rajesh for the meeting filled me with satisfaction. I looked her way, offering a friendly smile. Most of us have grown up seeing our fathers handing over an amount with which our mothers used to run the home while other investments and savings were always taken care of by the father only. Though this set-up has changed quite a lot in recent times, to date, investments and financial planning are considered to be "Men's departments" in most households. Ideally both partners should be involved in financial planning for their future for better planning and implementation. Let's understand why wives should also attend financial planning sessions with your advisor and husband.

<u>It Develops a Sense Of Mutual Understanding And Sharing Responsibilities Equally</u>

In most households, the responsibilities aren't equally divided between husband and wife. While the primary responsibility of a man in the household is to earn a living, the woman in the house takes care of all the household chores, kids, their caregiving, their studies, and managing the household budget. When you involve yourself in the financial planning process and also share your inputs about the same, you can help your partner and share his responsibilities. It helps develop a mutual understanding and also helps both of you understand whether you two are on the same page or not about financial goals. Both partners need to be on the same page for running a family and planning for its future. Moreover, when you take an interest in monetary matters and help your partner in the same, he may feel more responsible towards helping you in your role in the family.

You Get to Know the Financial Planner and About the Investments You Have

The most important reason to involve yourself in the financial planning process is to know about the family's financial goals and investments. It is common in our society that women in the house do not know about the investments their husbands have during any crisis. You can find many families paying off hospital bills and debts by selling jewellery when the husband is ill or no longer in the world. By involving yourself in financial planning along with your husband, you can jointly decide the financial goals and plan for the same and at the same time, you become aware of all the savings & investments that you and your husband are having. This helps a lot during a crisis. Moreover, it is essential to know your financial planner as well. This is crucial because you can deal with the financial planner, when the worst happens.

Otherwise, it becomes more difficult if you suddenly have to meet him, especially during a crisis.

<u>It Helps In Better Financial Planning And Implementation</u>

Women are regarded as born managers, have god-gifted management skills, and no one can manage budgets better than women. So, involving her in financial planning can be a wise decision for the entire family. Moreover, since women run the show at home in most cases, if they are unaware of finances, the financial planning and implementation of the same may not be aligned properly. So, visiting the financial planner along with your husband is important, and discussing household finances and regular investments is necessary to be on the same page. For instance, if your husband is planning to buy a car in the next two years and started investing in SIP, it is becoming difficult for him to manage other investments and this new SIP for the car. If you are aware of the same, you can downsize certain expenses at home which aren't necessary to help him save up easily for the car. This can only happen when you talk about your financial goals and household budget and mutually decide.

Final Thought

Whether you are an earning member or a homemaker, knowing about the finances is equally important for both partners. It is even important to include your child after they reach a certain age in these decisions so that they can understand the value of budgeting and investments from a young age. So, if you haven't gone to any of the meetings with the financial planner to date, make an effort to go from the next time onwards.

Understanding the challenges faced by busy entrepreneurs like Rajesh, I offered a solution, "Why don't you consider handing over a part of your investments to our Asset Management business's Portfolio Management Team? We specialize in managing substantial portfolios and can tailor our approach to your financial objectives and risk tolerance. This way, you can focus on your business, knowing that your investments are in expert hands. Our dedicated team will keep a close eye on market trends, rebalance your portfolio as needed, and ensure that your investments align with your goals."

I explained further, "A portfolio management service offers you the peace of mind that comes with professional management. Our team will take a holistic view of your investments and design a strategy that encompasses your entire financial picture. This service is especially beneficial for individuals with substantial portfolios, like yours. It allows for strategic decisions, risk mitigation, and proactive management."

Rajni nodded, contemplating the advantages of professional portfolio management. "Alright, Laxmi, let's move forward with your recommendation. I'll entrust my investments to Samruddhi Bank Asset Management's Portfolio Management Team."

Rajesh looked thoughtful for a moment and then inquired, "Can I start with a smaller amount for portfolio management initially? I'd like to develop trust over time."

I replied, "I appreciate your desire to build trust, Rajesh. However, I must inform you that the minimum amount to avail portfolio management services, as regulated by SEBI (Securities and Exchange Board of India), is 50 lakhs. This minimum requirement is not set by Samruddhi Bank but is a regulatory standard. While I understand that it may seem like a significant initial investment, it reflects our commitment to providing high-quality portfolio management services."

Rajesh considered this and then nodded in agreement, understanding the regulatory framework in place. "Alright, Laxmi, We'll start with 3 crores initially. I appreciate your guidance and look forward to having my investments professionally managed."

Certainly, I continued, "In addition, for your remaining investment portfolio, I urge you to seriously consider our recommended asset allocation. Learning the same lesson again isn't fun, especially with losses. Ignoring this advice might lead to a costly déjà vu."

As our conversation lightened, Rajesh, Rajni and I shared a laugh. They stood up, and we shook hands. I walked them to the door, and they left with a sense of understanding and agreement.

I returned to my desk and called our Corporate Communications head, who was discussing potential topics for our next media article. I had an idea in mind. Aman, our Corporate Communications head answers the call' "Hi Aman, so, I suggest we go ahead with an article on asset allocation, considering that many people lack awareness about asset allocation in their investments. I'll draft it soon. Please have your team proofread it before sending it to the media."

"Sounds good, Laxmi. Thanks for the idea! We'll make it happen." replies Aman.

I open Notepad on my laptop and begin jotting down my thoughts.

Don't Bet on Luck: Asset Allocation Beats Roulette

Imagine you're saving up for a dream vacation. Do you blindly throw all your money on red at the roulette table, hoping for a quick trip to Fiji? Of course not! That's pure gambling. Building wealth, be it for a vacation or any other goal, requires a smarter approach. Enter asset allocation.

Asset allocation is the foundation of any successful investment strategy. It's like packing for your trip – you wouldn't bring only swimsuits if there's a chance of rain. Similarly, asset allocation involves spreading your money across different investment types, like stocks, bonds, and cash. It's not about picking winners, but managing risk and aligning your investments with your goals.

Why Avoid Roulette Roulette?

Roulette is a game of chance. You might get lucky and win big, but the odds are stacked against you. The same goes for putting all your money in one asset class, like trendy tech stocks. A market downturn could leave you stranded financially.

Diversification: Your Investment Shield

Asset allocation acts as a shield against market volatility. Think of it like packing for all kinds of weather. By having a mix of stocks, bonds, and cash, you're hedging your bets. When stocks are down, bonds tend to rise, offering some protection. This diversification smooths out your overall returns, reducing the impact of dramatic ups and downs.

Finding Your Risk Comfort Zone

There's no one-size-fits-all approach to asset allocation. It depends on your age, risk tolerance, and goals. Someone saving for a down payment on a house might prioritize stability with more bonds. A young investor saving for a future car can afford more risk with stocks, potentially reaping greater rewards over time.

Don't Let Emotions Cloud Your Judgment

The market can be a wild ride. When stocks are soaring, it's easy to chase the hottest trends. When there's a downturn, panic can set in. A well-defined asset allocation strategy helps you stay calm and avoid impulsive decisions. It's your compass that keeps you pointed towards your goal, not the flashing lights of a roulette wheel.

Stay on Track with Regular Check-Ups

Your asset allocation shouldn't be set in stone. As your goals evolve and your risk tolerance changes, adjust your investment mix accordingly. Regularly review your portfolio and rebalance as needed to stay on track.

The Takeaway

Building wealth is a long-term game, not a gamble. Asset allocation may not be as flashy as roulette, but it's a far more reliable strategy to achieve your financial goals. By diversifying and staying disciplined, you'll be well on your way to securing that dream vacation (or whatever your goal may be!).

I copy-paste the entire text from Notepad to my mailbox and click the "send" button to forward it to Aman.

Annexure 1:

Stock Market Buffet

Imagine the stock market is a giant cafeteria serving up companies for you to invest in.

Large-cap Equities are the blue-plate specials. These are the Microsofts and Apples of the world, the established companies with a long track record of success. They're reliable, like mashed potatoes and gravy – maybe not exciting, but they'll fill you up and keep you steady. The downside? Their growth potential is kind of like a predictable side dish – tasty but not exactly surprising. Large-cap companies in India are usually ranked from the top 100.

Mid-cap stock Equities are the international food section. These are younger companies, maybe that hot new plant-based burger joint, with more room to grow. They offer a taste of something different, with a chance for higher returns. But be warned, these can be a bit spicier – there's a risk they might not survive the lunch rush. Mid-cap companies in India are usually ranked from the top 101-250.

Small-cap Equities are the food truck vendors parked way out back. These are the relatively tiny, unknown companies with the potential to be the next big thing. They're like a fusion food stall with exotic ingredients – you could end up with something delicious and innovative, or a flavor explosion that leaves you with heartburn. The risk is high, but the rewards can be outrageous. Mid-cap companies in India are usually ranked from the top 251 and above.

So, how do you choose your investment platter? It all depends on your appetite for adventure (and risk) in the investment world. Large-cap for stability, mid-cap for a balanced plate, and small-cap for a chance at something truly extraordinary (and maybe a little crazy).

Annexure 2:

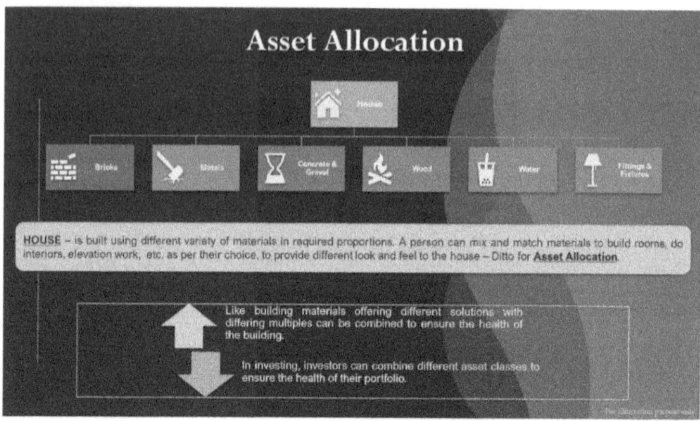

Asset Allocation
House
Bricks
Metals
Concrete & Gravel
Wood
Water
Fittings & Fixtures
HOUSE – is built using different variety of materials in required proportions. A person can mix and match materials to build rooms, do interiors, elevation work, etc. as per their choice, to provide different look and feel to the house – Ditto for Asset Allocation.
Like building materials offering different solutions with differing multiples can be combined to ensure the health of the building.
In investing, investors can combine different asset classes to ensure the health of their portfolio.

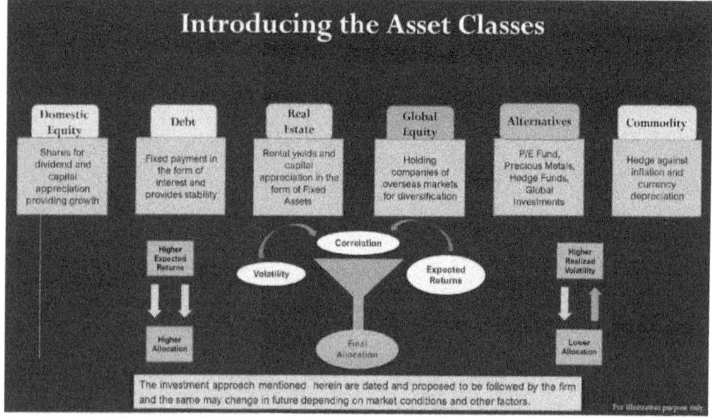

Introducing the Asset Classes
Domestic Equity
Shares for dividend and capital appreciation providing growth
Debt
Fixed payment in the form of interest and provides stability
Real Estate
Rental yields and capital appreciation in the form of Fixed Assets
Global Equity
Holding companies of overseas markets for diversification
Alternatives
P/E Fund, Precious Metals, Hedge Funds, Global Investments
Commodity
Hedge against inflation and currency depreciation
Higher Expected Returns
Higher Allocation
Volatility
Correlation
Expected Returns
Final Allocation
Higher Realized Volatility
Lower Allocation
The investment approach mentioned herein are dated and proposed to be followed by the firm and the same may change in future depending on market conditions and other factors.

CHAPTER 4

A NEW CHAPTER

SHE PEDDLED
ILLUSIONS OF
MY OWN DESIRES.

A gentle knock echoed through my cabin, and in walked Rajat. "Rhea has arrived," he informed. "Great! Send her in," I responded. Rhea entered with an air of confidence, her face portraying a readiness for the upcoming discussions. The navy-blue pantsuit added a touch of sophistication to her business-oriented appearance. The subtle click of her heels resonated with assurance, emphasizing her purposeful stride. A shared smile and warm handshake bridges the gap between us.

"Laxmi", I introduced myself to her, "Chief Investment Officer of this Samruddhi Bank."

"Myself, Rhea Kapoor", she introduced herself with a warm, welcoming smile. "Over the last three years, I've closely followed your LinkedIn posts & updates, Laxmi, and I must express how impactful your insights have been in shaping my investment journey. Inspired by your regular posts, I embarked on my investment journey with this bank. Your content brought a heightened awareness, offering valuable guidance on investment destinations, long-term planning, investment diversification and the significance of disciplined strategies. The focus on education and financial wisdom strongly resonated with me, leading me to explore the services offered by Samruddhi Bank.", continued Rhea.

I couldn't help but reflect on the profound impact that a trustworthy individual can have on shaping financial journeys. The connection established through shared insights and genuine expertise seemed to transcend the influence of a mere brand, creating a lasting impression on individual's financial choices and, consequently, their future.

Expressing gratitude for her kind words, I proceeded ''Thank you for your generous words, Rhea. I'm delighted to hear that my insights have played a role in shaping your investment journey. It's always encouraging to know that the information shared has been impactful for individuals like you who are navigating the complexities of financial planning and investment. Now, let's dive into the details of your portfolio and see how we can further optimize it for your financial goals. Moreover, we'll discuss your business loan application as well." "Ok", Rhea responded.

''Firstly, your systematic investment plans (SIPs) in mutual funds showcase a disciplined approach. The compounding effect is working well there. However, when it comes to your individual stock holdings, there's room for refinement. Diversification is a key principle to mitigate risks, and I noticed a concentration in a few sectors. By spreading your investments across various sectors, you not only reduce vulnerability to sector-specific risks but also position yourself to benefit from different market trends. Additionally, keeping a close eye on market trends and adjusting your stock portfolio accordingly can capitalize on emerging opportunities and shield against potential downturns. It's equally essential to grasp the duration you intend to hold onto a specific stock in the market."

"I appreciate your insights, Laxmi. I've been more inclined towards tech stocks due to their growth potential, but I understand the importance of diversification now. What would be the ideal approach to rebalance and diversify my stock portfolio?" questioned Rhea.

"Great question, Rhea. We'll start by identifying sectors that align with your risk tolerance and financial goals. Considering your tech-heavy portfolio, we can explore opportunities in other sectors like healthcare, finance, and consumer goods. Allocating a percentage of your stock portfolio to each sector helps distribute risk more evenly. Additionally, we can review your individual stock selections, considering factors like market trends, financial health, and growth potential. Regular reviews, typically on a quarterly or semi-annual basis, are crucial. Market conditions and individual stock performances can change, requiring adjustments. It ensures your portfolio stays aligned with your financial objectives. Rhea, to enhance your understanding of the market dynamics and potential investment opportunities, I recommend subscribing to Samruddhi Bank's weekly market update report and stock investment ideas report. These reports provide in-depth analyses of market trends, economic indicators, and specific stock recommendations. The weekly market update report offers a comprehensive overview of macroeconomic factors, industry trends, and market sentiments. Understanding these elements helps you make informed decisions about your investments. On the other hand, the stock investment ideas report delves into detailed studies of specific companies, offering insights into their financial health, growth prospects, and potential risks." I explained

"That sounds valuable. How do I subscribe to these reports?" inquires Rhea.

"As a Samruddhi Bank client, you have exclusive access to these reports. I'll connect you with our client services team, and they will ensure that you receive these reports regularly. Incorporating these detailed analyses into your research process will further empower you to make strategic investment decisions." I continue. "Remember, staying well-informed is key to navigating the dynamic landscape of the stock market. If you have any questions along the way, feel free to reach out."

Rhea flashed a grateful smile and remarked, "I appreciate your guidance, Laxmi. Thanks, a tonne".

Once the basics were covered, I leaned forward, signalling my genuine interest. "Now, Rhea, tell me about your business plan. I'm eager to hear your vision, your unique value proposition in the fashion industry, and your long-term goals."

Moving on to our discussion about the business loan, after covering the initial groundwork. "Rhea, you may have received an email from the bank yesterday informing you that we couldn't approve your business loan."

Rhea, visibly disappointed, nodded and replied, "Yes, I did receive the email. I was hoping for a different outcome."

"Ms. Kapoor, I appreciate your enthusiasm and commitment to your entrepreneurial endeavours. However, after a meticulous evaluation of your loan application, I must convey that the bank is unable to approve the loan at this juncture. Several key factors contribute to this decision, and I want to provide you with transparent insights.

Firstly, your current monthly income projections doesn't meet the minimum threshold required to support a loan of 2 crores. The stringent financial criteria we adhere to necessitate a certain level of income stability to mitigate risks associated with significant loans. Additionally, your relatively young age and limited professional experience contribute to the perceived risk in approving such a substantial loan.

I understand this might be disheartening news, but our commitment is to ensure the financial well-being of our clients. It's crucial to consider your financial stability and experience before undertaking loans of this magnitude. I'm here to assist you in understanding these factors better and explore potential avenues for the future. I noticed in the email that you're planning to launch a fashion brand named GreenStyle. Why don't you tell me about your business plan. I'm eager to hear about your vision, the unique value proposition GreenStyle brings to the fashion industry, and your long-term goals."

Rhea begins to speak with zeal and passion, "GreenStyle was born out of my passion for fashion and a deep concern for the environmental impact of the fashion industry. The fashion world is constantly evolving, and I saw an opportunity to revolutionize it by integrating technology and sustainability. GreenStyle will be a virtual Wardrobe Styling App. I aspire for a physical store too in the future. However, for now, even the loan intended for marketing and other essential app operations faced a setback. So for now, the Virtual Wardrobe Styling App is our flagship offering. It employs advanced AI to analyze user preferences, taking into account current trends and budget constraints. Users can initiate the shopping process by capturing a full-length photo within the app. Subsequently, they have the flexibility to select any garment of their choice, visualizing how it would appear on them through the app. Additionally, they can experiment with pairing different outfits and accessories before making a purchase, ensuring a personalized and informed shopping experience.

Our AI-powered Fashion Analysis is intriguing. The AI system is the backbone of our platform. It not only considers user preferences but also aligns with their personal style and financial considerations. This sets us apart, offering a personalized and intelligent wardrobe solution. The result is a personalized and curated selection of clothing items, ensuring that users not only look good but also make eco-conscious choices. Our Sustainable Fashion Marketplace is a key component. I've curated a selection of brands that share our commitment to ethical and sustainable practices. Through strategic partnerships, we offer users a diverse range of options, allowing customers to make choices that align with their values. Our emphasis on Fashion Sustainability Tracking is noteworthy. It empower users to make ethical choices.

Our platform allows users to track the environmental and social impact of their purchases, providing insights into the lifecycle of each garment. It fosters responsible consumerism, contributing to a more sustainable and ethical fashion industry. We will cater to the growing demand for responsible fashion choices."

Rhea delivered the entire monologue in one breath. The deluge of information hit me like a tidal wave – a bit much to process all at once.

Seeing my puzzled expression, I guess Rhea understood my struggle to comprehend. She explains further, "I have a detailed company profile ready, and I'll email it to you. But, I've got an important call with my HoD at 5:30 PM that I can't skip. I need to rush."

"Sure," I responded as Rhea hurriedly got up to leave. I stood up to shake hands. "I'll be waiting for your email.

Thank you for your time, Rhea." Rhea shook hand, smiled and left.

The conversation concluded in a slightly unusual manner. Anyways, as soon as Rhea left, my office assistant brought in a platter of fresh fruits and a glass of coconut water, something he does every evening. It might seem simple, but it meant a lot. It's not just about the fruits; it's a break in the middle of all the financial talks. These small acts of kindness, I felt grateful for a team that values these gestures, giving me a moment to recharge amid all the finance discussions.

I savored the fruits for a bit before returning to my emails. Rhea's company profile had quietly landed in my inbox during the break. I opened the attachment, and there unfolded Rhea's company profile as follows -

Company Profile: GreenStyle

Introduction:

GreenStyle is a pioneering force in the fashion industry, combining cutting-edge technology with a commitment to sustainability. Our core mission is to provide users with a revolutionary fashion experience that seamlessly blends style with eco-conscious choices. At GreenStyle, we believe in the power of fashion to make a positive impact on the world, and our innovative solutions reflect this belief.

Our Identity:

GreenStyle captures the essence of our brand – an intersection where style meets sustainability. We are not just a fashion platform; we are a movement towards a greener and more conscious future. Our commitment to environmental responsibility and trendsetting style defines the very fabric of our identity.

The GreenStyle Experience:

1. Virtual Wardrobe Styling App:

At the heart of our offerings is the GreenStyle Virtual Wardrobe Styling App. This sophisticated application leverages artificial intelligence to analyze user preferences, current trends, and budget constraints. The result is a personalized and curated selection of clothing items, ensuring that users not only look good but feel good about their choices. This user-centric approach to virtual styling sets GreenStyle apart in the competitive landscape, offering a unique and enjoyable shopping experience.

2. Sustainable Fashion Marketplace:

GreenStyle is dedicated to promoting sustainable and eco-friendly fashion. Our marketplace serves as a gateway for users to connect with a carefully curated selection of brands that share our commitment to ethical and sustainable practices. Through strategic partnerships, we bring users a diverse range of options, allowing them to make choices that align with their values. By actively seeking collaborations with leading sustainable brands, we aim to be at the forefront of the sustainable fashion movement.

3. AI-Powered Fashion Analysis:

Our advanced AI system is the backbone of our Virtual Wardrobe Styling App. GreenStyle's AI-driven approach redefines fashion-tech, making our platform a go-to destination for those who seek a personalized and intelligent wardrobe solution.

4. Fashion Sustainability Tracking:

Transparency and accountability are fundamental values at GreenStyle. Our platform allows users to track the environmental and social impact of their clothing purchases. By providing detailed insights into the lifecycle of each garment, we empower users to make choices that resonate with their values. This unique feature fosters responsible consumerism, enabling users to contribute to a more sustainable and ethical fashion industry.

Market Requirements for Sustainable Fashion:

1. Rising Environmental Awareness:

In recent years, there has been a significant increase in environmental awareness among consumers. People are becoming more conscious of the environmental impact of their choices, including their fashion purchases. As a result, there is a growing demand for sustainable fashion options that allow individuals to express their style without compromising their environmental values.

2. Ethical Consumerism:

Consumers are increasingly seeking brands that align with their ethical values. The demand for transparency in the fashion industry has led to a shift in consumer behavior, with individuals actively seeking out brands that prioritize ethical sourcing, fair labor practices, and sustainable production methods. GreenStyle caters to this demand by curating a marketplace that features brands committed to ethical and sustainable practices.

3. Technological Integration:

As technology continues to advance, consumers are increasingly looking for innovative solutions that enhance their lifestyle. GreenStyle's use of artificial intelligence to analyze fashion trends and user preferences positions the platform at the forefront of technological integration in the fashion industry. This not only meets the expectations of tech-savvy consumers but also sets a new standard for fashion-tech platforms.

4. Desire for Fashion with a Purpose:

Modern consumers are seeking products and experiences that go beyond aesthetics. There is a growing desire for fashion with a purpose, where each purchase contributes to a greater cause. GreenStyle addresses this need by not only offering stylish and trendy options but also by allowing users to track the environmental and social impact of their fashion choices. This feature will add a meaningful dimension to the fashion experience, resonating with consumers who want their choices to make a positive difference.

Conclusion:

GreenStyle is not just a company; it's a movement towards a more sustainable and conscious fashion future. Our commitment to combining style with sustainability positions us as a leader in the industry, catering to the evolving needs and values of the modern consumer. As we continue to innovate and expand our offerings, we invite fashion enthusiasts and eco-conscious consumers alike to join us on this journey towards a greener and more stylish world.

This felt like a lot of theoretical information, and I craved something practical. Spotting Rhea's number in her email signature, I dialled it. "Hello," Rhea answered. "Hi Rhea, Laxmi here. Just a quick question, have you started developing the app?" "Yes," Rhea replied. "I'm already 80% there. The only thing left is a partnership with brands."

"Awesome," I responded. "So, Rhea, any plans for tomorrow? It's Saturday, after all." "Yeah," she said, "weekend mode on." I chuckled, "I suppose tech folks get a break on weekends." Rhea laughed, "Guilty as charged. What's up?" "How about we see your app tomorrow?" I suggested. Rhea countered, "Sure, but are you processing my loan?" "No," I replied, "different agenda. I'll fill you in. What do you say?" "Alright," Rhea agreed after a brief pause. "Sounds interesting," she added. "Great," I said, "I'll WhatsApp time and venue. Let's catch up based on our mutual availability." ''Alright, see you tomorrow" Rhea replied.

As the conversation with Rhea ended, the evening took its course. My phone chimed with a notification that never failed to bring a smile – a message from Pranav, my husband. His message reassured our dinner plans: "Picking you up at 7 PM. Can't wait to see you after a long and exhausting day."

"OK" I reverted.

FROM RED WINE TO RED TAPES

LOVE, A TENDER BLOOM, OFTEN FINDS ITSELF CHOKED
BY THE THORNS OF DECEIT
IN THE GARDEN OF COMMERCE & BUSINESS.

United by dreams of making a difference, Pranav and I first crossed paths during our college first year. Our connection blossomed into a cute love story that stood the test of time. As the years unfolded, so did our shared dreams.

Together, we founded a women-oriented Trust, a financial haven crafted for and run by women, Sahyogini Financial Trust.

I embarked on my professional journey at the age of 22, joining Samruddhi Bank as a Trainee Investment Counselor. Eight years ago, Pranav and I also established a trust with the mission to empower women financially. Our collective vision resonated strongly, garnering notice from Samruddhi Bank, which later emerged as the trust's largest benefactor. Subsequently, I became Managing Trustee for the trust, and through a series of promotions, I eventually attained the position of Chief Investment Officer at Samruddhi Bank.

However, a pivotal moment arose when donors' pressure coerced Pranav to make the difficult decision to leave the Trust. The donors sought a more profit-centric approach, deviating from the Trust's original ethos.

True to his words, Pranav arrived near my office gate exactly at 7 PM. The restaurant he selected; "Fallow" was renowned for its subtle elegance. As we entered the softly lit space, a gentle jazz melody enveloped the air, setting the stage for an intimate evening.

Pranav was dressed in a white shirt with an ochre-coloured check collar, exuding a perfect blend of casual charm and refined style. His choice of cologne lingered, leaving a subtle and enticing trail as he moved. His personality, as always, radiated warmth and confidence, creating an inviting atmosphere for the evening ahead.

The waiter guided us to a cozy corner table adorned with fresh flowers and flickering candles. The menu showcased a range of exquisite Italian dishes, each a masterpiece in its own right. Pranav and I immersed ourselves in a symphony of flavours, relishing every bite of the pasta. A bottle of rich red wine complemented our dinner, infusing additional warmth into the already enchanting atmosphere.

As we enjoyed our meal, I turned to Pranav and asked, "How was your day at work, Pranav?"

Pranav's expression carried a weight of disappointment as he sighed and began to share, "Today was quite challenging, Laxmi. We had put forward an application, aiming to take our company public. However, things didn't go as planned, and the application faced rejection. It was a crucial moment for us, especially during an investor meeting where the pressure was intense. The setback came as a blow, adding a layer of difficulty to an already demanding day. We were hopeful about the expansion, and opportunities going public could bring; but now we need to reassess our strategy and find a way forward despite this setback. " I exclaimed in disbelief, "Oh, what reasons did they mention for rejecting the application?"

Pranav began to elaborate on the reasons behind the rejection, "Laxmi, our application faced rejection due to a combination of factors. One significant aspect was pending or unresolved legal issues that our company is currently entangled in. This includes ongoing lawsuits and regulatory investigations that haven't been fully addressed. The regulatory authorities are strict in their scrutiny, and any outstanding legal matters can act as a significant barrier to approval. Let me give you an example of one of the legal issues that played a role in our rejection. We manufacture medical devices, and there was a lawsuit filed against us by a former employee who claimed an injury caused by one of our products. This lawsuit has been lingering, and while we believe it lacks merit, the fact that it's unresolved became a red flag during the application review. The regulatory authorities scrutinize such cases closely, and until we can conclusively address and resolve these legal matters, our path to approval remains challenging."

He continued, "Another critical factor was the failure to adequately disclose material legal risks in our application. The regulatory bodies demand transparent and thorough disclosure of any potential legal risks associated with the company's operations. Unfortunately, it seems we fell short in providing a comprehensive overview, and this inadequacy contributed to the rejection. Nevertheless, I'm currently in the process of recruiting a skilled compliance team, and I'm also in discussions with one or two prominent lawyers. I hope we can resolve these issues soon, allowing us to reapply."

Pranav's expression reflected the weight of these issues, highlighting the complexity and challenges involved in navigating the regulatory landscape for a public listing.

"Consider me a resource, Pranav. If there's anything you need assistance with, I'm more than willing to help." I offered. Pranav nodded, a subtle smile playing on his lips as he gracefully poured another round of wine into our glasses, the rich red liquid gliding smoothly and filling the crystal-clear goblets. The soft glow of the candles reflected in the wine, creating a warm ambiance that mirrored the growing intimacy between us.

Pranav gazed at me with a warm smile and remarked, "You know, there's something about the way red suits you. It's not just a colour; it enhances your natural grace and adds an extra layer of elegance to your presence. Truly, you look absolutely stunning in red." He commented further, "Oh my god! Just look at those pink blushing cheeks. If blushing were an Olympic sport, you'd be a gold medalist by now." I was just blushing uncontrollably; Pranav rarely showered me with compliments. He had maintained his stubborn demeanour since our college days, making this unexpected praise all the more special.

I responded with a playful touch of humor, "Um-hmm, apparently my pink cheeks are on a mission to match my red outfit."

As the wine gradually worked its magic, I felt a surge of confidence, prompting me to delve into a more serious conversation. With a sincere expression, I turned to Pranav and said, "You know, Pranav, I've been thinking. Sahyogini Trust is taking a new direction, focusing on the principles we initially set – a financial haven for and by women. It made me reflect on our journey and the dreams we shared."

I observed the shift in Pranav's facial expressions, and he responded, "Laxmi, can we please not discuss this topic right now?"

Pausing for a moment, I continued, "I understand why you had to step away when Bank took over Sahoyogini. The investor pressure must have been immense. But Pranav, the trust needs you. It needs the vision we crafted together. I want to propose something – join the trust again, Pranav. Be part of this transformation. We can make it even more impactful than we ever imagined."

Pranav expressed with frustration, "Laxmi, it's disheartening to see how Sahyogini has deviated from its original vision. The essence of empowering women seems diluted, especially with your bank's involvement. One instance that truly frustrated me was when, as the Managing Trustee of Sahyogini, you and Samruddhi bank's board of directors approved a 15-18% interest rate on loans for women-owned SMEs. Charging such a high interest rate contradicts the very idea of empowering women. How does imposing a 18% interest rate align with our vision? You & I initially agreed that the interest rate for women-owned SMEs wouldn't exceed 8 to 10%. This decision was crucial to support and uplift women entrepreneurs, ensuring fair and reasonable financial terms. The sudden shift to a 18% interest rate contradicts the principles we set in place and raises concerns about the bank's commitment to its original vision."

I pacified Pranav and began to clarify, "Pranav, you need to understand the circumstances. When Samruddhi Bank started dominating Sahyogini, we were in dire need of funds. Bank was the biggest donor, and we had to comply with their terms. But now, 60% donations are done by me pesonally, I can make independent decisions as I serve the largest capital to the trust. I'm in the process of reevaluating all the models and projects of Sahyogini, including the interest rates. We'll address and rectify these issues. I need your support in this endeavour. After all, Sahyogini started because of you, inspired by your mother. Think over it, take all the time you need to reflect on it and decide what feels right for you."

CHAPTER 6

FROM WRINKLES TO PRENUPTIAL WRINKLES

PRENUPS ARE LIKE ORDERING A PIZZA WITH
A PRE-DETERMINED CHEESE DISTRIBUTION.
NO FIGHTING OVER THE SLICE
WITH EXTRA MOZZARELLA IN THE FUTURE!

The next morning, I reached out to Rhea Kapoor on WhatsApp, checking her availability to meet up at 1 PM. I recommended a charming European coffee shop with a delightful German bakery in Worli. I had a skin boosters' appointment at my best friend Manisha's clinic for 10 AM. She's been persistently urging me to undergo this treatment to bid farewell to the fine lines and wrinkles on my face. Ah, the joys of the finance world – where the hustle never sleeps, and apparently, neither does the aging process. According to Manisha, my finance-fueled lifestyle has magically transformed me into a sophisticated 50-year-old, though I'm still basking in the glory of my mid-30s. So, here I am, diving into my first facial hydrofilling session, accompanied by a delightful gossip session with my ever-enthusiastic buddy, Manisha.

As I make my way to Manisha's clinic, I open my laptop in the car. Usually, I receive numerous investor queries through various media houses. During the weekends, I start writing answers to address these inquiries.

Following was the first question -

Does low-cost companies represent good investment opportunities?

Response **Not necessarily.**

While low-cost companies (based on stock price) can be tempting, a strong investment opportunity requires a deeper examination than just affordability. Here's why:

- **Price Alone Does Not Tell the Story:** A low stock price (like our example of Company X at ₹15) might seem like a steal, but it could indicate underlying issues. These could include declining revenue, high debt, or an outdated business model.

- **P/E Ratio Offers Context:** The price-to-earnings (P/E) ratio is a key metric to consider alongside stock price. It compares a company's stock price to its earnings per share. A low P/E ratio (relative to the industry average) for a low-cost stock could be a sign of an undervalued company with good growth potential.

- **Temporary Challenges vs. Long-Term Woes:** Sometimes, a low stock price and P/E might reflect temporary setbacks, like regulatory changes (Company X's example again). Savvy investors can identify these situations and potentially find hidden gems.

The Flip Side: High-Cost Stocks Can Be Winners Too

Don't automatically dismiss high-cost stocks. If a company has strong earnings and growth justifying the high price point, it could still be a great investment.

The Key: Comprehensive Due Diligence

Regardless of stock price, smart investing requires thorough research. This helps you differentiate between:

- **Undervalued Opportunities:** These low-cost stocks with low P/E ratios might be on the upswing.

- **Value Traps:** These low-cost stocks with low P/E ratios might seem attractive but have fundamental problems justifying the low price (e.g., potential for long-term decline).

Similarly, high-cost stocks with high P/E ratios might be justified by the company's strong financials and future growth prospects.

The Bottom Line:

Focus on a company's fundamentals, not just the stock price. Conduct a comprehensive analysis to understand the factors influencing both price and P/E ratio. This will help you make informed investment decisions and avoid potential value traps.

The moment I wrap up my response, my phone buzzes with a confirmation text from Rhea for our 1 PM catch-up. We reached the clinic, and as I exit the car, I shift my attention to the driver and inform him, "Ramesh Ji aaj 1 baje Worli jaana hai. Idhar se direct chale jayenge."

As soon as I walked into the clinic, I informed the receptionist, "Please let Manisha know that Laxmi has arrived." While awaiting Manisha, I observed the clinic staff—stunning women with radiant, glass-like skin, their faces glowing with extravagance. Manisha has certainly excelled in in-clinic marketing.

Stepping out of the cabin, Manisha greets me enthusiastically, exclaiming, "Hiiiiiiiiiiiiiiiiiiiiiiiiiii, Laxmi!" and gestures with open arms, ready for a friendly hug. Manisha, the undisputed champion in the "Volume Olympics." She's basically the decibel queen of our social circle. She is so loud.

"Hi," I respond back with a grin. Manisha, as expected, fires a playful jab, "You are always dull and boring." I continue, "Well, someone has to maintain the zen balance around here. By the way, start your hydrofilling thingy fast; I need to rush. I have a meeting at 1." Manisha raised an eyebrow and frowned, "Time's always chasing you darling, isn't it? Tea or coffee?"

I replied, "Green tea, please." Manisha instructs one of her staff to fetch me green tea, and we make our way to the Manisha's cabin. Manisha was going through a divorce battle with her husband, and I suddenly realized I hadn't spoken to her about this issue in months.

As we settled down and one of Manisha's staff served me green tea, I asked her, "How's your divorce case going? Have you officially divorced, or is the case still ongoing?"

Manisha sighed and responded, "Yeah, still in the process. It's stuck over alimony, yaar. I have the responsibility of raising two young kids. I'll have their custody. The alimony is primarily for their well-being."

I remarked, " Certainly, the responsibility of raising children is shared equally by both parents, regardless of whether they are together or not."

Alimony, also known as spousal support or maintenance, is a legal obligation for higher earning spouse to provide financial support to the other after a divorce or separation. Its purpose is to address the economic disparities between spouses, ensuring that the lower-earning or non-earning spouse can maintain a standard of living similar to that enjoyed during the marriage. Alimony is typically granted when there is a significant financial discrepancy between the spouses, and its duration and amount are determined based on various factors, including the length of the marriage, the financial contributions of each spouse, and the recipient's needs.

While alimony serves a crucial role in promoting financial fairness, it is essential not to take it for granted or misuse it. The recipient should use alimony responsibly, focusing on rebuilding their life and financial independence. Similarly, the payer of alimony should fulfill their obligation with integrity, recognizing that it is a legal and moral commitment. Misusing alimony, such as withholding financial information or using it for purposes other than intended, undermines the purpose of this support system. Respect for the legal process and open communication between former spouses are vital to ensure that alimony serves its intended purpose of providing financial stability during a challenging transition.

Manisha continues further, "Touchwood, Laxmi, your marriage is going very well, and may no evil eye fall upon it. But let's consider a hypothetical scenario – if you were to part ways with Pranav and take custody of Ruhi, would you ever consider seeking alimony for her well-being? After all, both of you share a joint responsibility for her as parents."

"Pranav and I signed a prenuptial agreement, commonly known as a prenup, several months before tying the knot. In case of separation, our financial responsibilities toward each other are predetermined as per the terms of that agreement," I explained.

Manisha raised an eyebrow, countering, "Prenupital? But Indian laws don't really acknowledge prenuptial agreements..."

I replied, "Yes, in India, the concept of a prenuptial agreement doesn't hold legal validity as marriages are regarded as sacred and not merely contractual. However, one can still document and register the terms under the Indian Contract Act, treating it like any other contractual agreement. It's crucial to address these issues beforehand to avoid complications later on. A well-drafted agreement covering items, gifts, and the amount of permanent alimony can provide clarity and prevent disputes. It's wise to consider property matters, especially in cases of joint ownership, and determine the share of each spouse upfront. Creating a comprehensive agreement, duly witnessed and registered, is a prudent step to ensure a smooth and fair resolution if the need arises in the future. Though Pranav and I were confident about our marriage, and did not hold any ill intentions.. but in case unfortunate circumstances arise, the purpose of such agreements is to mitigate the financial stress and trauma that individuals often endure during separations." Manisha remarked, "Well, that was a smart move."

Manisha exclaimed, "Alright, enough about me. Let's head to the procedure room and kickstart your hydrofilling treatment. Let's give you that glass skin!"

While heading to the procedure room, I express a mix of nervousness and excitement. Seeking clarity on the upcoming treatment, I turn to Manisha and ask, "Can you refresh my memory about the specifics of the procedure? I remember bits from our discussion when I visited your clinic last time, you examined my skin" Manisha explains, "Certainly! We'll be using Restylane Skinboosters, a Hyaluronic acid-based product. It involves a micro-injection technique, delivering hyaluronic acid into the skin to enhance hydration, plumpness, and smoothness for damaged or dull skin. Due to continuous exposure to factors like pollution, sun, air conditioning, and heating appliances, the natural hyaluronic acid in the skin diminishes, leading to roughness, dullness, fine lines, and loss of elasticity. The Restylane Skin Boosters treatment addresses these concerns by replenishing lost hyaluronic acid and collagen, hydrating the skin from within. This results in a plumper and rejuvenated skin texture. Moreover, these booster shots will specifically target your sagging skin on cheeks, and under-eye areas, providing a visible tightening effect."

I recline on the clinical bed in the procedure room, observing as Manisha and her team put on their surgical gloves gear up for the procedure. The crinkling sound of the injection packaging and the meticulous arrangement of tools on the surgical tray make me tad nervous. "I must admit, the idea of those injections are scaring me to death now," I confess to Manisha.

" Relax, Laxmi. The numbing cream we apply beforehand makes the treatment nearly painless. Afterward, you'll notice a natural glow on your skin, and it will appear more refreshed, hydrated, and youthful. You'll absolutely fall in love with your skin," assures Manisha. Manisha, accompanied by another staff member, began creating a grid-like structure on my face. Once my skin was adequately numbed, they initiated the process of injecting tiny, votile injections into each square of the grid. Typically, there was approximately one injection per square maybe. "After the procedure, you may experience mild redness and swelling for a few hours, but you'll be completely fine by tomorrow," assured Manisha during the treatment. The entire procedure took approximately 45 minutes to an hour. After cleaning my face, she mentioned, "You will need two more sessions." Handing me a mirror, she asked, "How do you feel?" As I gazed into the mirror, I couldn't deny that I felt good.

"Thank you, Manisha. I appreciate this radiant and glass-like skin, even if it's artificially achieved," I expressed.

"Why consider it artificial? If you perceive it that way, you won't fully enjoy the benefits of this session. Opting for this skin booster shot was a proactive measure to seize control over the aging process, fostering a sense of empowerment and self-determination. The mind and body are interconnected. Positive changes in your physical appearance, like enhanced skin texture, can positively influence your mental well-being, creating a harmonious mind-body connection," Manisha explained.

I nodded and asked Manisha, "Are we finished?" as her assistant began wrapping up. Manisha responded, "Yes, want to grab lunch?"

"Next weekend, Manisha, please. I already have a working lunch planned for today at 1 pm," I said. "Okay, no problem. Just a reminder, you may or may not experience a little irritation on your skin. Just be relaxed about it; it will be fine in a few hours," said Manisha. "Okay, and when will the next session be?" I asked as I called my driver to pick me up. "Three weeks," replied Manisha as she came to see me off until I got into my car. I was 15 minutes late, and as soon as I entered the cafe, I noticed Rhea already sitting at the corner table, engrossed in her laptop.

Annexure

The Arranged Prenup: Why You Should Discuss the Undiscussable in Indian Marriages

Love marriages or arranged marriages, the idea of a prenuptial agreement (prenup) in India can raise eyebrows faster than a Bollywood dance number. But here's the truth: prenups aren't just for Hollywood celebrities. In the land of shaadi bells and elaborate ceremonies, a prenup can be a surprisingly progressive tool for modern Indian couples.

Why the Hesitation? Let's Debunk the Narratives!

Unromantic?

Love is about trust, but trust thrives with clear communication. A prenup is a chance to openly discuss finances, a topic often tiptoed around. It shows maturity and a desire to navigate any future bumps together, even financial ones.

Un-Indian?

Traditionally, marriages were about families coming together, not dividing assets. However, with changing times and increasing financial independence, prenups can ensure fairness and respect individual contributions.

Enforceable?

A well-drafted prenup with full disclosure may be considered favourably during a divorce settlement. It acts as a pre-discussed agreement, promoting a more amicable resolution.

So, when do people consider a Prenup?

Protecting Your Legacy: Inherited a family business or have a thriving career? A prenup safeguards your pre-marital assets, ensuring they stay within your family or are divided fairly.

Debt Reality Check: Carrying student loans or a family loan for the wedding? A prenup clarifies how these liabilities will be handled, avoiding future arguments.

Blended Family Blues: Entering a marriage with children? A prenup can specify inheritance rights and ensure everyone is financially secure.

Transparency for Entrepreneurs: One partner runs a startup? A prenup can protect the other's interests while acknowledging the entrepreneur's potential future earnings.

How to Make the Prenup a Powerhouse of Positivity

Communication is Key: Don't spring the prenup bomb! Discuss it openly, maybe over a relaxed dinner. Explain it as a way to solidify your commitment and build financial security together.

Get Legal Expertise: Involve a lawyer specializing in family law. They'll draft a prenup that's fair, protects both parties, and is considered valid in an Indian court.

Focus on the Future - Frame the discussion as planning for a long and happy marriage, but also acknowledging that life can take unexpected turns.

A prenup or prenuptial agreement isn't a shield against love, it's a safety net for unforeseen circumstances. It allows you to step into your married life with open hearts, clear finances, and the knowledge that even if the path changes, you'll navigate it together.

CHAPTER 7

MEETING A SHE-EO

THE CURRENT CROP OF YOUNGSTERS ARE ALL BUDDING CHESS GRANDMASTERS, WHILE THE REST OF US ARE STILL TRYING TO FIGURE OUT HOW TO PLAY CHECKERS. WHAT AN AGE TO BE ALIVE !!!

I greeted Rhea with an apology for being late. As a courtesy, Rhea stood up for a handshake. As we took our seats, I suggested, "Let's order some food first; I'm starving." Amidst the aroma of freshly brewed coffee and the allure of delectable pastries, antique wooden chairs that invited patrons to sink into their comfort as they savored my favorites, from rich, aromatic espressos to the buttery, melt-in-your-mouth croissants, we settled down for a butter croissant with jam and hazelnut coffee.

"Shall we dive into the app now?" I inquired with Rhea. "Certainly, are you using an Android or iOS phone?" Rhea asked. "Android," I replied. "Great, you can find Greenstyle on the Google Play Store. It's already live," Rhea informed. Excitedly, I searched for Greenstyle on the Play Store, confirmed the app with Rhea, and installed it. After finishing the installation, I turned to Rhea, saying, "Done." Rhea pulled her chair next to me, ready to assist. "Okay, you can start filling in the details required for signing up on the app now," Rhea instructed.

I proceeded to fill in the required information on the app, starting with my full name, gender, email ID, and phone number, all verified with OTP. The app then prompted me to set up a password and touch sensor for fingerprint login. The final step involved entering a captcha, with two tick boxes for accepting marketing preferences and the terms of service and privacy policy agreement. Both boxes needed to be checked for the "Let's get started" button to be enabled. Turning to Rhea, I commented,

"Having the privacy policy box mandatory makes sense, but marketing preferences should be optional." Rhea agreed and noted it down in her diary. Curious about the privacy policy, I asked Rhea if she had involved a compliance person. She replied, "No, it is yet to be drafted. It's an empty document right now." "Okay," I said, redirecting my attention to the app.

I encountered two pop-ups for notification preferences and location information, choosing the "allow only while using the app" option. Once onboarded, the app prompted me to take a full photo. Rhea explained, "You need to take a photo or selfie here, and the app will automatically style clothes on you. It's a one-time process, and the algorithm sets your size for all the clothes on the app."

I asked Rhea to take my photo, and she clicked my pictured and hits the upload button. I was then directed to the shopping page. Rhea shared, "Currently, I have onboarded two brands whose clothes and accessories you will see. Both brands are environmentally friendly Indian homegrown clothing brands that supported me in integrating their products on my app. Both these brands are into eco-friendly apparels manufacturing, belonging to people whom I have met, interacted, and built a network through in-person engagements, fostering lasting connections".

To my surprise, on the shopping page, all the clothes were not styled on like other shopping apps. Instead, everything was styled on my avatar, generated by AI. The images were accurate and realistic, making the shopping experience more personalized. I expressed my excitement, noting that this approach allowed me to make purchases based on how the items looked on me rather than on models. Upon first viewing the clothes, the clothes were styled on me. As I swiped right, I saw the same items styled on models for a more realistic representation of the product. I complimented Rhea, saying, "This avatar are most hyper-realistic avatars, Rhea. Most avatars I've seen appear cartoonish, but these looks remarkably authentic."

Rhea thanked with a subtle smile. As I scrolled down the selected product, I came across a comprehensive product description. The size, automatically chosen based on my uploaded picture, was remarkably accurate. I even had the option to select a different size if needed, right beside the chosen one. Adjacent to that was a convenient size chart. Further down, I found detailed information about the product, including its authenticity, product code, manufacturer details, seller information, and an option to explore more products from the same brand. Below that, I discovered styling ideas for the chosen dark blue kurti with golden jardoshi work.

The styling recommendations encompassed matching pants, dupattas, earrings, necklaces, and more, all coordinated with the blue kurti. Each item was styled in line with my avatars, allowing me to choose the one that best appealed to me. I clicked on a particular avatar, and it displayed all the products that were paired together. I had the option to purchase each item individually or add the entire ensemble to the cart with a single click. All the clothing items and accessories featured on the app, whether for men, women, or kids, were crafted exclusively from environmentally friendly materials such as organic cotton, linen, hemp, khadi, vegan leather, ecovero, etc. Additionally, I had the option to select apparels based on the material of my choice. Upon clicking the "khadi" filter on the left, I could easily view all the outfits made from khadi across thesebrands.

I had a variety of sustainability features to choose from, including options such as handlooms and handicrafts, organic materials, natural dyes, eco-friendly choices (Regenerative Agriculture), vegan products, cruelty-free options, and water-saving, Carbon Offsetting, Energy-Efficient Production, Zero-Waste Design, Upcycling and Repurposing alternatives.

I inquired, "Can you explain the water-saving filter and how it applies to clothing?" "Water-saving filters focus on clothing items produced with dyeing processes that use minimal water or waterless techniques, aiming to reduce water consumption and pollution," Rhea explained. Continuing the discussion, I asked, "And what does the 'Regenerative Agriculture' filter entail?" "It shows products from brands utilizing materials sourced from regenerative farming practices, which aim to improve soil health, enhance biodiversity, and sequester carbon." answered Rhea. Rhea added, "Let me demonstrate another intriguing feature."

Rhea taps on the "My Impacts" button in the menu bar. Users have the option to access the carbon footprint calculator and also track the environmental and social impact of their clothing purchases on the app.

Rhea explains, "Let's explore the carbon footprint calculator. Let's say you want to buy that blue kurta, a matching golden bottom, and a dupatta. To start, enter the product codes for each item. The app has already stored information about the sustainability features of the garments, such as whether they are made from organic cotton, recycled polyester, or other eco-friendly materials. Manufacturing process details, like traditional or sustainable methods, are also accounted for.

Next, select the delivery address, and the calculator considers transportation emissions from the seller's location to yours using geolocation. As the next step, you'll then estimate the product's longevity and how you plan to dispose of it, whether through recycling, donating, or disposal. The app employs a predefined algorithm based on life cycle assessment (LCA) principles, calculating the overall carbon footprint by summing up emissions from material production, manufacturing, transportation, use, and end-of-life.

I'll input some rough details to demonstrate, and now, let's hit 'Calculate' The app displays the calculated carbon footprint in a user-friendly format, showing a numerical value and a visual graph. It provides information on how this purchase impacts the environment and even compares the carbon footprint to other similar items or industry averages. Also, once you make a purchase on the app, it will display Social Impact Metrics, showcasing the positive impact you've made. Unfortunately, the payment transaction and purchase completion pages are yet to be coded, so I can't demonstrate it now.

These metrics will highlight the social impact of your purchase, for e.g. support for fair wages, community development, or charitable contributions associated with that particular product purchase. This information will be permanently stored on the app and can be viewed under the 'My Impacts' page. Each product purchased will be accompanied by impact metrics, giving you a comprehensive view of the positive change associated with each item."

Rhea continues, "We also have something to attract the new generation. You know, whatever the younger generation, like me, does is to impress people on social media. So here we go with one more feature. You can share your look on social media. Now, this app has already curated a look for you, clothes are styled well on your avatar. Let's go back to your blue kurti. Can you please click on that product?"

I follow Rhea's instructions and open that product again. Rhea continues, "Below the Sustainability rating of that particular product, there is a button called 'share this look.' Can you please click that?" I click on the button, and a drawer opens from the bottom, asking me on which social media app I want to share this look. Rhea says, "Please click on WhatsApp and share this look with me." I continue doing as she says. Rhea opens her WhatsApp. On WhatsApp, she receives that particular product styled on my avatar, and there is one link attached to it at the bottom. She turns her phone towards me and opens the link. She gets an option to vote for that look – with a like, dislike, and average button. She clicks on like. As soon as she likes it, I receive an app notification on my phone saying 'Rhea Kapoor likes your look.' On my app, I see 1 like on that look. Rhea further says, "People can share these styled avatars with their friends or relatives. They can decide whether they want to purchase this product based on the likes they receive or other factors if they consider."

Rhea shares, "We have one more exciting feature on the app. You can send your used clothes to us for upcycling. You'll find that feature under the 'My Profile' section. Please click on your profile on the top left and choose 'Donate Clothes for Upcycling.' Once you click on that option, you'll have to add details like the material of the clothes, the number of clothes you'll be donating, the address for pick up, and a suitable date and time. Our delivery agent will go to the user's location and collect the clothes. We will then send these clothes to our partnered brands who manufacture apparels by upcycling old clothes. In return, users will earn reward points for reducing clothing waste, where 1 reward point equals 0.25 rupees."

I interrupt Rhea, "I have a question here. On what basis will you onboard a brand? How will you identify how truly sustainable they are?"

Rhea responds, "We have a thorough vetting process for onboarding brands onto the app. Firstly, we assess their sourcing practices, ensuring they use sustainable materials like organic cotton, linen, hemp, khadi, vegan leather, and more. We also look at their manufacturing processes, giving preference to brands with low-impact and eco-friendly manufacturing. Transparency is key, so we verify that brands have clear supply chain information and ethical production practices. Additionally, we consider certifications and partnerships with recognized sustainability organizations & assess the management team's experience and track record. Only brands that align with our commitment to environmental and social responsibility make it onto Greenstyle." I inquire further, "What types of certifications are considered?" Rhea elaborates, "We prioritize brands with recognized certifications that validate their commitment to sustainability. Some of the certifications we look for include Global Organic Textile Standard (GOTS) for organic textiles, Fair Trade for ethical and fair labor practices, and certifications specific to eco-friendly and cruelty-free materials. These certifications serve as tangible proof of a brand's dedication to environmentally conscious and socially responsible practices." I complimented Rhea, saying, "These features are truly impressive, Rhea. The design and UI are exceptionally elegant. Fantastic job!"

Rhea expresses, "I've put in a lot of effort into the app, Laxmi. Unfortunately, my business loan application was rejected, and now I'm facing challenges with funds for operations and marketing. My parents provided some initial support for setting up this business, but they can't contribute further. Despite considering applying to other banks, the rejection from Samruddhi Bank has been disheartening. I had hoped that with the current global economic conditions, especially the challenging economic situation in the US, loans would be available at lower interest rates, making it an opportune time for funding. However, it seems like a difficult situation right now."

I countered, "Yeah, there is a challenging economic situation in certain areas of the world, but India remains relatively unaffected. We might not witness significant changes in interest rates, and there may not be any major macroeconomic effects. We are standing strong." Rhea asked further, "How did the Indian economy manage to do that? Many economies across the world are getting affected."

I answered, " In contrast to the high challenging economic situation experienced by the American economy this year, the Indian economy remained largely unaffected. This resilience can be attributed to the average Indian's proclivity for saving and a lifestyle characterized by reduced reliance on credit and debt, distinguishing it from other parts of the world. The macroeconomic advantages of this financial behaviour contribute significantly to stability. The elevated savings rates prevalent among Indians play a pivotal role in bolstering the financial system's stability. This surplus of savings provides banks with increased lending capacity, thereby diminishing the risk of financial crises The impact extends to the resilience of the population in the face of economic shocks. India's high savings rate also translates into a reduced dependence on foreign capital for investment endeavours. This self-sufficiency fosters economic independence, shielding the country from the volatility associated with global financial market fluctuations. In essence, the Indian economy's ability to weather the global economic challenges of the past year underscores the advantageous macroeconomic effects of a population inclined toward savings and a judicious avoidance of excessive credit and debt. Moreover, these higher savings are not merely idle funds; they serve as a wellspring for investments, benefiting both individuals and institutions. I'm not stating that this is the sole reason, but indeed, it could be one of the factors."

Rhea commented, "Yes, that could be true. But now unfortunately, especially the young population, are transitioning to credit cards and falling prey of Buy Now Pay Later services, leading to an increase in debts with substantial amounts tied up in outstanding balances in India."

I was pleased that Rhea understands all these aspects. In contrast, today's youth tend to adopt a different strategy. They increasingly accumulate debt and rely heavily on credit, resulting in a surge in outstanding credit card balances quarter after quarter. An illustration of this shift is that over 70% of iPhone purchases in India are made through EMIs. Moreover, even online shopping platforms, particularly those specializing in luxury products, have enticed more customers by offering high-end clothing on EMIs, making luxury purchases more accessible. This shift signifies a departure from the traditional asset-first approach to a more immediate gratification-oriented lifestyle.

Times have changed, and the concept of lifestyle inflation is creeping into the younger generation's mindset. The pressures of social media, the allure of influencers flaunting opulent lives, are reshaping spending patterns. It is as if the pursuit of a grand lifestyle has overshadowed the importance of prudent financial planning. When you scroll through Instagram and come across a fashion blogger's 'Get Ready With Me' reel, you'll often spot luxury brand containers or bags strategically placed on their background shelves. It's a way of showcasing their ownership of something from renowned names like Louis Vuitton, Chanel, or Gucci, even if they aren't actually wearing those brands in the reel. It's a subtle form of flaunting, designed to give viewers FOMO (Fear of Missing Out).

Modern-day advertisements are masterfully crafted to create a sense of opulence, making you feel like you're missing out on something monumental if you don't own a particular item. Our young Indian generation is particularly susceptible to this influence. Influencers hold a certain power over their audience, often invoking the reciprocity norm, where people feel obliged to return favours.

In this context, influencers can leverage this norm to encourage their followers to purchase products from specific brands. It's worth noting that sometimes, even the clothing featured in these influencer reels isn't something they can genuinely afford. They may buy the clothes, create the reel, and then return the items to the store or claim they don't need them anymore, especially if they purchased them online. Authenticity in such promotions is a rare find, as most influencers prioritize the allure of luxury over genuine endorsement.

The next challenge to tackle is Lifestyle Inflation. This occurs when non-essential spending increases along with income. It's a common pitfall, especially for millennials and Gen Z, who may feel pressure to match their peers' lifestyles. The urge to upgrade one's wardrobe or indulge in cosmetics is often driven by this inflation. Lifestyle inflation and unchecked spending habits can have broader economic consequences. When individuals consistently increase their non-essential spending as their income grows, it leads to a rise in consumer spending overall.

This surge in consumer spending can potentially impact inflation rates within the economy. Inflation occurs when the prices of goods and services increase over time. If a large portion of the population is engaging in lifestyle inflation and spending excessively on non-essential items, it can contribute to overall rising prices. This is because increased consumer demand for these non-essential items can drive up their prices due to limited supply.

Moreover, lifestyle inflation can also contribute to income inequality within the country. Those who are able to control their spending and invest wisely tend to accumulate more wealth over time. In contrast, individuals who succumb to lifestyle inflation and spend impulsively may struggle to build savings or investments. This wealth disparity can lead to a significant income gap between different segments of the population.

I took the last sip of my coffee and said, "Anyway, let's refocus on GreenStyle. So, Rhea, instead of heading to banks and seeking loans, have you considered pitching GreenStyle to an angel investor? You could secure investment without accumulating debt and, in return, offer equity of your company to the investor. It's a way to fuel growth without the financial burden of traditional loans.".

Rhea paused and replied, 'Well, actually, I've been thinking about maintaining autonomy for the business. Pitching to investors can be a lengthy process with too many rejections, and, honestly, I have an impatient mind. I thought by obtaining OPC status, it would be easier for me to secure a business loan and have the flexibility to manage the company without diluting equity too much.'

I nodded, understanding her perspective and replied "But, Considering the option of angel investors for GreenStyle could be a game-changer. These investors don't just provide funds for your business; they bring in their experience and helpful connections. This support can fast-track company's growth, helping it expand and stay competitive.

Secondly, choosing not to take out loans has its perks for GreenStyle. It means steering clear of regular payments and repayments, providing more flexibility with the company's cash. This flexibility is crucial, especially during uncertain economic times.

Being free from the burden of debt allows the company to be more adaptable in its financial approach. You can use profits to reinvest in the business, explore new opportunities, and maintain a solid financial position.

This kind of flexibility is like having a financial safety net, helping GreenStyle navigate challenges and make the most of growth opportunities while staying financially healthy."

Rhea nodded and added, "I agree; that makes sense. However, pitching my idea to an investor will take a lot of time. I'm almost done with the app, and now I need to shift my focus to forming strategic partnerships. Hunting for investors would eat into that time, especially with my full-time job on the plate."

I responded, "If the challenge lies in pitching to investors and not equity dilution, I believe I can offer some help.."

Intrigued, Rhea questioned, "Help as in finding an investor?"

Leaning in, I replied, "What if I say the one is sitting right in front of you."

Rhea arched an eyebrow, a sly smile forming on her face as she shifted her focus to her buttery croissant, delicately slicing it with her knife. Curious about the change in her expression, I asked, "What happened?"

Rhea explained, "I had a hint of something like this when you proposed a meetup, especially on a non-working day, even after the bank rejected my loan."

The current crop of youngsters are all budding chess grandmasters, while the rest of us are still trying to figure out how to play checkers. What an age to be alive!!!

Rhea inquired, "What are your thoughts on my business idea and the work I've put into this app?"

I replied, "Absolutely fantastic. I was truly captivated by the app, especially the feature that showcased clothes on me rather than just models. It's refreshing to envision what looks good on oneself. Also, your commitment to sustainable practices is commendable. You might even qualify for specific incentives or tax benefits tied to eco-friendly initiatives. Investing in such forward-thinking startups seems like a no-brainer; it could revolutionize the fashion industry."

Rhea inquired, "Thanks, Laxmi. How much are you considering to invest, and what percentage of equity are you looking for?"

For a moment there, it felt like I accidentally stumbled into my own interview.. suddenly I felt like I was in the hot seat.

I inquired, "Firstly, have you registered your company as an OPC, a One Person Company?" Rhea replied, "Yes, it's an OPC. Initially, I wanted autonomy, so I had to choose between sole proprietorship and OPC. In a sole proprietorship, I would have had unlimited liability, I'd be personally responsible for all debts and legal obligations of the business. With OPC, my liability is limited to the extent of my investment in the company, safeguarding my personal assets from business liabilities." I nodded and remarked, "True, smart thinking." I continued further, "And how much have you currently invested in the company?"

"50 lakhs," Rhea replied, "a blend of my savings and a dash of parental support."

"Certainly. In terms of financial requirements, what is the projected investment needed to establish and sustain the business successfully?" I queried. Rhea responded, "An estimated 5 crores, to maintain operational efficiency for the initial 2-3 years, in the absence of immediate profit generation."

I replied, "That's a big amount. The most I can contribute is 3 crores, of course subject to the approvals as per the regulatory and bank's internal governance that I am required to as a senior employee. Of course, I won't be blindly handing over the funds. I'd need a clear understanding of how effectively you plan to manage this investment. Could you provide insights into how the funds will be utilized in one report and share details on the current financial status reflected in your books?" Rhea responded, "Sure, give me a couple of days, and I'll send you a detailed report. If all goes as planned, and you decide to invest in GreenStyle, what percentage of equity would you be looking for in return for your investment?"

I responded, "Look, Rhea, determining the price per equity share is a process intricately tied to the company's valuation. The valuation itself involves several factors such as comparable company analysis, discounted cash flow analysis, book value, etc. However, considering GreenStyle is a Pre-Revenue Startup, let's simplify this. Now, you've already put in 50 lakhs, and if I invest 3 crores. To calculate my equity stake, we can use my capital contribution, which is 3.2 crores divided by the total investment in the firm, 3.5 crores. The math gives us roughly 85.7% when converted to a percentage. But, and here's the crucial part, let's not apply strict math here. After all, it's your brains and efforts behind GreenStyle. I'd prefer moving forward with a 60% stake."

"Alright, that seems reasonable," Rhea replied.

Rhea, while having a commendable vision for her company and showcasing remarkable work on the app, seemed to lack the maturity needed to navigate the intricacies of running a business. Though I sensed she placed some trust in my guidance, it struck me that if she were pitching to another any angel investor, the allure of a high valuation might have been tempting. However, it could potentially lead to overvaluing her company, presenting challenges in subsequent funding rounds and impacting investor expectations.

During our conversation, I noticed a lack of contingency planning on her part. Failing to anticipate and plan for unexpected challenges can be detrimental to a startup's success. Operational and team challenges, such as effective management, hiring, and scalable processes, were crucial aspects overlooked. This neglect might have made it challenging for her to secure any other investors' confidence.

Moreover, the importance of regulatory compliance was seemingly underestimated in her project plan. Ignoring regulatory requirements can result in legal complications, and startups should prioritize adherence to relevant laws in their industry.

The absence of burn rate management raised concerns. A sudden influx of capital without proper budgeting and control could lead to increased spending, risking the longevity of the funds and hindering the achievement of meaningful milestones.

Strategic alignment between the startup's vision and what are my goals as an investor was not addressed by her. Ensuring compatibility is crucial to avoid conflicts in the future. It's essential to choose investors who comprehend and support the long-term vision of the company.

Lastly, she didn't inquire my potential exit strategies, or the returns I expected. These aspects are pivotal for establishing a strategic partnership and aligning expectations between investors and founders.

Recognizing the gaps in Rhea's business management approach and foreseeing potential challenges, I felt compelled to proactively step in and guide Rhea toward the long-term success of GreenStyle. Despite being a first-time angel investor, my primary focus should have been on securing attractive returns given the high risk involved. However, I couldn't ignore the burning desire in Rhea—her relentless effort and strategic approach toward realizing the goals of GreenStyle.

Reflecting on my own journey at 25, I shared a similar vision of establishing my own business, as is common for many now-a-days. Yet, what stood out in Rhea was the confidence I once lacked. While she undoubtedly requires significant guidance, and her current planning may fall short for the success of GreenStyle, I wanted to extend my support. Both of us are embarking on a substantial risk this time, and I see this as an opportunity to not only potentially gain returns but also to mentor and empower a determined entrepreneur like Rhea.

Rhea inquired, "Laxmi, I've registered GreenStyle as an OPC, but OPC rules state that there can only be one shareholder. How can I give you a shareholding?"

I clarified, "According to MCA rules, if the capital surpasses 50 lakhs in One Person Company, we must mandatorily convert the company to a Pvt Ltd regardless of how long it has been registered. For voluntary conversion, if the capital does not exceed 50 lakhs within two years or if the annual turnover does not surpass 2 crores, we are required to wait for a mandatory two-year period before converting from OPC to Pvt Ltd. However, if the capital exceeds 50 lakhs before two years or the annual turnover reaches 2 crores, mandatory conversion is required. Moreover, it's generally advisable to have a Pvt Ltd company or LLP instead of an OPC.U A Pvt Ltd structure offers several advantages, including increased credibility, better access to funding opportunities, and enhanced scalability. Pvt Ltd companies can have multiple shareholders, allowing for broader ownership and easier transfer of shares. Additionally, the mandatory conversion threshold for Pvt Ltd companies provides a more stable and versatile legal structure for long-term business growth compared to the limitations imposed by OPC regulations. My suggestion is to incorporate both a Pvt Ltd and an LLP. One Person Companies (OPCs) are limited to a single shareholder."

Nevertheless, Rhea curiously asked, "How can we make that happen?"

Continuing my explanation, I removed the dairy and pen from my purse and commenced scribbling down my thoughts, "Let's consider we have two different entities, GreenStyle Pvt Ltd and GreenStyle LLP. GreenStyle Pvt Ltd will be responsible for managing the e-commerce app, overseeing product listings, customer transactions, and fulfillment, as well as engaging in marketing and promotions to drive sales. On the other hand, GreenStyle LLP will focus on sustainability assessments and partnerships, actively collaborating with sustainable fashion brands, conducting due diligence on potential partners, and providing reports and recommendations for integration decisions. The products of these partners will only be listed on the app when Greenstly LLP gives green signal to Greenstyle Pvt Ltd. The LLP will also stay attuned to industry trends, updating sustainability criteria accordingly.

Now, envision a reserve fund of 3.5 crores within GreenStyle LLP, with a clearly specified percentage of shareholding for both partners. GreenStyle Pvt Ltd will have the flexibility to secure loans from GreenStyle LLP for operational needs. This will be governed by a formal agreement detailing terms, interest rates, and repayment schedules. Profits generated by GreenStyle Pvt Ltd will be shared with GreenStyle LLP, fostering the overall financial health of the partnership, and a well-defined profit-sharing model will be established."

"The reason I suggest having two entities is because GreenStyle LLP promotes sustainable practices and assesses brands based on environmental standards. If we adopt additional sustainable measures, such as accepting only digital payments to eliminate paper transactions and using electric scooters for deliveries to reduce carbon emissions, GreenStyle becomes eligible for corporate income tax deductions under section 80JJA. This means we can cut down on taxes.

Even though the profits will be generated by Pvt Ltd, there will be profit sharing between LLP and Pvt Ltd. The partners in LLP will also serve as directors in both companies—LLP and Pvt Ltd. While I'm not an expert in this area, seeking legal advice from tax professionals will be essential to ensure everything aligns with regulations and is in our best interest."

"Oh, this is now interesting" remarked Rhea.

Rhea, with a sense of realization and gratitude, expressed, "You know, Laxmi, today's revelation was quite eye-opening for me. I came to understand that I've been navigating the intricacies of running a company with only a fraction of the knowledge required – not even 25% to be precise. That's when it struck me how crucial having a mentor like you is going to be on this journey."

She continued, "Your dual role as a promoter and mentor makes you exceptionally valuable to me. Your in-depth understanding of the industry and market dynamics is something I'm eager to tap into. With your guidance, I'm hopeful that I'll gain a better understanding of risk management and how to adapt to market changes. I see your mentorship going beyond the business aspects, impacting my personal development as well. Your insights into leadership, decision-making, and professional growth are something I'll eagerly anticipate. Laxmi, thank you for being such an integral part of this journey, guiding me selflessly and generously. I will be truly fortunate to have you as both a promoter and a mentor."

I chimed in with a playful one, "Oh, but my dear, you won't be getting the keys to the kingdom that easily. Securing access to the 3 crores won't be a walk in the park. You'll need to articulate a convincing plan on how you intend to utilize these funds efficiently. I await your well-crafted proposal. Consider it a little challenge—your pitch, please!"

"Certainly, I will send it within the next couple of days," Rhea responded.

I inquire, "Have you initiated any hiring processes so far?" Rhea mentioned, "Not at the moment, but I am currently seeing one freelancer for strategic partnerships with fashion brands. It's the immediate requirement. That guy seems skilled, but there's a bit of a struggle within the budget constraints for bringing him on board."

I remarked, "Indeed, a crucial hire, as much of the groundwork for your app is completed. Now, it's about bringing on board partners whose products can be featured. Can I meet him?"

I also wanted to see the kind of people Rhea is hiring. The team she puts together right now will be really important for the company's growth. After all, the heart of a company lies in its core team, for it is they who steer and drive the growth of the entire organization.

"Sure, I will request him for an in-person meeting and coordinate a gathering at a time convenient for all three of us."

I expressed, "Thank you, Rhea. I'll have to take my leave now. Once again, great job on the app." Rhea extended her gratitude as I signalled the waiter for the bill.

UNFINISHED CONVERSATIONS HAUNT THE FUTURE

"BIRTHDAY TRIP TO AMSTERDAM? SWEET! JUST REMEMBER, HONEY, WHILE YOU'RE 'SEALING THE DEAL" WITH MR. BIGSHOT, I'LL BE CONQUERING THE CANALS... SOLO.

Future

As I hop into the car to head home, I give Pranav a call and gently remind him, "Hey, it's your turn to take Ruhi to her skating session today." Pranav, with an apologetic tone, admits, "Oh, it totally slipped my mind." Feeling a bit frustrated, my voice unintentionally gets a tad louder, "Come on, Pranav. Juggling responsibilities isn't easy for me every time. Ruhi is your daughter too. Am I the only one responsible for her schedules?"

Pranav calmly responds, "Just a heads up, it's already 4:30 PM pm. The skating sessions were from 2:30 pm to3:30 PM, and Ruhi and I are already back home after a wonderful session. I've told you countless times to work on your impulsive reactions."

"Alright, my mistake. But seriously, what an impulsive reaction on my part! I got all worked up thinking you missed the session, yaar." I replied.

Pranav commented, " That was quite a spur-of-the-moment reaction, typically the way women often do, right?"

"Pranav, that's absurd and misogynist, a typical masculine mindset. I reacted that way because I didn't realize it was already 4:30 PM" I said.

"Alright, my bad. I am sorry," Pranav admitted.

"Fine. Anyway, I need to discuss something. I'll be home in a bit." I said.

Pranav reassures, "Cool, even I have something interesting to share." Intrigued, I inquire, "What is it?" Pranav playfully responds, "Well, you'll find out once you're back home. Let's catch up then!"

I finally arrive home after getting stuck in the mind-numbing traffic. Dealing with this daily traffic has become a routine, and it's seriously taking a toll on my mental energy.

Upon reaching home, I spot Ruhi with a colourful karaoke mic in hand, singing "Baby Shark Doo doo doo doo" at an ear-piercing volume. I rush to Pranav, exclaiming, "Who got her this annoying thing? Now she won't give up, and I'll be serenaded with 'Baby Shark' all day. Plus, it's so darn loud!"

Pranav responds, "I got it for her on our way back from her skating classes."

Perplexed, I ask, "Whyyyyyy?" Pranav explains, "Well, she really wanted it. We found it near her skating class, and Ruhi's friend's mom got for her daughter. Ruhi saw that and then she also desperately wanted that. I've never refused Ruhi and even you for anything EVER!"

With a frown, I retort, "Okay, fine, as a symbol of love, you might as well build the Taj Mahal. You've never objected to anything, right?" Pranav chuckles and says,

"Haha, Taj Mahal and a symbol of love. Well, Shah Jahan had other wives besides Mumtaz, and some even claim he married Mumtaz's sister after her death. Should I still build a Taj Mahal?"

"Good heavens, could one of you please be quiet now? Honestly, I'd appreciate it if both of you could just hush." I said. Pranav gently holds me and says, "Alright, relax. Let's head to the balcony. I'll get you some wine and cheese. You mentioned wanting to discuss something, right?" "Yeah," I reply with a slightly paling face, and we make our way to the balcony. Pranav joins me there with two glasses of rosé wine and a platter full of baby Swiss cheese, crackers, and some chocolate-covered berries.

I take a sip of the rosé wine and to appreciate it's flavours, I proceed to nibble on the cheese.

"So, I've been meeting this girl, Rhea Kapoor, for the past two days. I won't dive into the intricacies of how we met or the detailed story behind her startup, but I'm genuinely impressed by her business idea and the current progress she's made. It's unique, creative, and definitely worth investing in," I shared.

"Okay?" Pranav inquired. " Her focus is on building an e-commerce platform where users can seamlessly shop for fashion apparel with a strong commitment to environmental friendliness. While she may not have the maturity to handle a business, the app she has developed has a potential to spread like wildfire in the market, I feel.

I am planning to invest around 3 crores in her business." I explained.

"So, exploring angel investing, I see. That's a great move! It will be a much-needed breath of fresh air from the monotony of your mundane wealth management job. " Pranav uttered, lighting his cigarette.

"Is it in very early stages, or is the startup already up and running?" Pranav inquired, taking a drag from his cigarette. "Yeah, she's yet to go live, it's in very pre-mature stage" I informed. "Well, it's a significant risk with your money then," Pranav remarked. "I understand that, but I trust in her passion. Besides, she'll have my full-time support as a mentor to navigate the business and delve into its intricacies," I explained.

"I understand that you have a good sense of reading and understanding people's competence levels. If your instincts suggest potential, there might be something there. However, I do have another option where you can play it a bit safer," Pranav said. "What option?" I inquired. "Signing a Full Ratchet anti-dilution agreement," Pranav suggested.

"Oh, but opting for a full ratchet could present several disadvantages for Rhea in the future, especially if her business faces any downturns or if she needs to secure additional funding," I remarked.

"Pranav, we need to tread carefully here. Just because Rhea is new to all this doesn't mean we should take undue advantage. If, after a year or so, she discovers the consequences and realizes we didn't explain everything properly, she might lose faith in me. It could seem unfair, and she may think we've been selfish due to her ignorance. Remember, a real queen fixes another queen's crown without telling the world it was crooked. We should operate with integrity and transparency in our dealings with Rhea. In line with this, I suggest we opt for a weighted average anti-dilution agreement. It not only safeguards our interests but also ensures fairness and equity in the long run. It encourages us to offer support and guidance without exploiting her inexperience, fostering a positive and empowering dynamic".

Pranav responded, " Yeah, makes sense! I was just asking to keep yourself on the safer side since it will be your very first time for angel investing. And, of course, it's a significant risk, so you shouldn't get demotivated by it. Otherwise, a weighted average anti-dilution is always the better and most commonly used option. Before committing, why not seek advice from your mentor, Rekha Ji?"

I remarked, "Exactly my plan. I'll reach out to Rekha Ji, probably tomorrow or the day after, and get her insights on it." Pranav remarked, "So, if you remember, I mentioned I have something to share." I responded, "Oh, yes. Please go ahead."

Pranav mentioned, "So, I told you next to next week is your birthday week, and you are keeping yourself free for the entire week." I rolled my eyes and replied, "Yes, love, I remember. You've reminded me about it a hundred times, and I've made sure not to schedule anything during that time. My calendar is wide open." "Excellent," Pranav remarks.

"Perfect," Pranav acknowledges, gracefully removing an envelope from his pyjama pockets and handling it over to me. "What's inside?" I inquire, accepting the envelope and unfolding it with a curiously.

There were 4-5 printouts within, each one unveiling a fragment of a dream. Flight tickets for both of us to Netherlands, a Schengen Visa, and tickets to the Van Gogh Museum. My joy couldn't be contained, for it had been a dream that harboured for almost two decades—to wander amidst the artistry of Van Gogh. He, the maestro who ignited my passion for art & uncovering emotions in creativity within me, and here I stood, a devoted Van Gogh enthusiast.

"Seriously?" I ask Pranav, my eyes misty, overwhelmed with gratitude and excitement.

"We're heading to the Netherlands for two reasons—firstly, obviously yes, naturally to celebrate you and your enchantment with Van Gogh, and secondly, I have a business meeting," Pranav shares.

"What's the business meeting about?" I inquire.

"Exciting news, indeed. We've secured a foreign direct investment from a Netherlands-based investor to bolster our company's Electronic Health Record (EHR) facilities, particularly in rural and underserved areas. While our medical devices with integrated EHR software are already top-notch, their efficiency in rural settings needs a boost. We're planning to leverage satellite technology to enhance software connectivity in these underserved regions. Additionally, we're venturing into the manufacturing of medical delivery drones. Just envision the impact during the COVID times—having a sufficient fleet of these drones could significantly reduce mortality rates," Pranav enthusiastically shared.

"Is it not possible to import medical devices with enhanced EHR technology?" I inquire from Pranav. He responds, "We do import them, but the majority end up either idle or poorly functioning. Devices imported from developed nations often exhibit a 99% inefficiency due to their lack of suitability for our environment."

Pranav, with a sense of pride, shares an example of venture into manufacturing cutting-edge medical devices: "Take, for instance, our 'CogniCare Neural Interface.' It's a marvel, integrating neural technology with Electronic Health Records to redefine healthcare. This device excels at functions like real-time brain activity monitoring, molecular-level vital sign tracking, emotion analytics, auto-documentation of symptoms, predictive health modelling, remote consultations, and emergency response coordination. Imagine the capability to capture real-time brain activity, providing unprecedented insights into cognitive functions for the early detection of neurological disorders. Move beyond traditional vital signs—this device delves into molecular-level monitoring, detecting anomalies at a cellular level to uncover hidden health issues. "

However, Pranav acknowledges a significant challenge: "Despite the brilliance of these devices, we've faced hurdles in rural areas. The 'CogniCare' was initially designed with an urban environment in mind, where high-speed internet and advanced infrastructure are prevalent. But in rural areas, the lack of robust connectivity has hindered the device's seamless operation. We're now actively working on a version tailored for these underserved regions, incorporating satellite technology to ensure efficient functioning even in remote locations."

"Do you see where the crux of the issue lies?" Pranav remarks, lighting up another cigarette. A palpable sense of disappointment reflects on his face. "Even though we're capable of generating significant income, the business is yet to achieve profitability. I'm still failing to figure out whether it's due to unmanaged debt levels, cash flow problems, unexpected expenses, or mismanagement of funds. Just can't understand what could it be?"

I find it puzzling that, despite my ability to easily spot issues by examining the company's books, Pranav has never regarded me as a potential resource for his business. While I don't want to interfere unnecessarily, he rarely shares updates on both the positive and challenging aspects of his business.

"Hmm," I murmur. "Ever thought about bringing in a CFO?" Pranav ponders, "Yeah, that might be the best move now."

"Hire me," I suggest. Pranav laughs, "Wait, what?"

I repeat, "Hire me. I'm already done with this CIO role. Let's build the business together. I can take care of your investor relations, manage cash flows, sort out fund mismanagement—whatever financial needs you've got, count on me. I just need a break from Samruddhi Bank. I'll handle the Sahyogini trust, and we can be business partners."

Pranav laughs again, saying, "You're kidding." "I'm serious," I insist, puzzled by Pranav's reaction. "Okay, we can talk about that later. Right now, let's head inside and grab some dinner. I'm starving," Pranav suggests, collecting the plates and wine glasses as he heads back to the living room.

As I proposed the idea of becoming business partners with Pranav, his skeptical reaction raised my suspicions. The laughter and dismissive tone felt more than just surprise; it seemed like there might be something he's not expressing openly. It's making me wonder if there's a hidden layer or concern that he's not sharing. The decision to postpone the discussion adds to the uncertainty, leaving me suspicious about what could be going on in Pranav's mind. I'll need to approach our future conversations with a curious yet cautious mindset to unravel the truth behind his reactions. Or else, it's possible that he needs time to wrap his head around the idea of transitioning our personal relationship into a business partnership and I am just overthinking. Anyways!

FINANCE DIVAS

PARENTS' MEDICAL BILLS
SCHOOL FEES RECEIPT
COMPANY'S FINANCIAL DOCUMENTS
HOUSEHOLD BUDGETS
HEALTH INSURANCE POLICY

It's a fine Sunday morning, I make my way to Sahyogini's office. You know, the grind never takes a day off for our amazing staff, voluntarily working all seven days a week at the Trust. While en route, I decide to dial up Rekha ji, the heart and soul of our Trust, who is leading our Individual Grant Programmes division. She promptly picks up, and I pop the question, "Rekha ji, are you coming to office today? Wanted to discuss something".

With a chuckle, she replies, "Of course, Laxmi! Weekends are like a foreign language to seasoned folks like me. What's there to do for someone at my age? Might as well spend the time doing something exciting. Ab iss umar mein kya hi karungi.. But Madam, I need to know, are you planning to grace the office with your presence? It seems like sometimes it slips out of your mind that you are the Managing Trustee."

"Coming, coming! I apologize for my absence from the office for the past three weeks. I've been juggling a lot of things, not that I'm making excuses. However, I trust the reins of the Trust are securely in your hands, so I'm super confident the shop won't be burned down," I explained.

"Alright, come on in. We've been waiting for you," Rekha ji replied.

Upon my arrival at the office, the staff welcomed me warmly, and there stood Rekha ji, ready to greet me. This workplace is one where I genuinely enjoy being — dedicated to social causes, raising awareness, and nurturing women's personal growth. As I made my way to my cabin, an employee from the medical grant division hurried over, seeking my signature on a medical grant agreement for someone named Mrs. Renuka Devi.

Curious about the financial aspect, I inquired, "How much is the grant for?" She promptly responded, "5 Lakhs." Concerned about the availability of funds, I asked, "But do we have enough funds to support such grants repeatedly? Grants are subject to the availability of funds, right?" She replied, "Yes," seemingly unsure.

"Anyways, hand me the agreement for the time being. I'll review it and decide what needs to be done," I said, taking the agreement and heading into my cabin. Settling down, I called for a cup of hibiscus green tea. Just then, Rekha ji strolled into my cabin, saying, "And here she is, our Finance Diva!"

"Finance diva?" I exclaimed. "Yes, indeed, that's you!" she replied with a smile, pulling up a chair to join me. Rekha ji chuckled and explained, "You manage to make finances look glamorous and effortless. Hence, the title – Finance Diva!" She continued, "You bring a certain flair to numbers that not everyone can, and we all appreciate that. So, embrace your Finance Diva persona!"

I couldn't help but smile at Rekha ji's playful characterization. "Well, if being a Finance Diva means making finances look glamorous, I suppose I'll gladly embrace the title," I said with a hint of humor. "Let's keep the numbers dancing to our tune and continue making a positive impact through our financial endeavours."

"Haha, Right. By the way, did you get this agreement for Renuka Devi's Medical grant?" Rekha ji asked.

"Yes, just received it. The amount of 5 lakhs seems quite substantial right now, especially given that Samruddhi bank is reducing the percentage of donations every quarter. Due to this, I am forced to increase my contributions each quarter to counterbalance that. However, sustaining such significant amounts for an extended period will be challenging. We might consider offering concessions on hospital bills through our affiliated hospitals or guiding her towards charitable hospitals. Unfortunately, a grant of 5 lakhs won't be feasible, Rekha Ji. Last year, we distributed a total of 3 crores for both medical and educational grants. However, this year, Samruddhi bank's contributions are diminishing significantly, and the donor intent is dwindling. Our priority now should be on fundraising," I explained, my patience wearing thin.

"Laxmi, the issue is, she doesn't have health insurance. I feel sorry for her. Moreover, being a widow, Renuka couldn't benefit from her husband's life insurance after his demise. Renuka and her husband purchased a home five years ago through a home loan with a repayment term of 15 years. Unfortunately, they didn't invest in mortgage life insurance to safeguard their home loan. Tragically, Renuka's husband passed away last year, marking the fourth year of the repayment period. Currently, Renuka is struggling to make ends meet, unable to afford basic necessities and responsible for caring for her two minor children. Adding to her challenges, creditors have the primary claim on her husband's policy proceeds in the event of his death." Rekha ji explained.

In the intricate tapestry of life, women play pivotal roles as caregivers, breadwinners, and homemakers. Understanding the nuances of insurance is crucial for women to navigate the complexities of modern life with financial confidence.

"Fundraising seems like the obvious solution at the moment, but I wanted to get your perspective." I told Rekha ji.

"Laxmi, we should explore collaborations with corporates that have active CSR committees. It can significantly boost our funds and resources." Rekhaji emphasized.

"I agree, that's a sound suggestion," I remarked.

"Many corporations are eager to contribute to social causes. We identify those whose values align with ours, pitch our mission, and propose a collaboration. It's not just about funds; it's about leveraging their resources and networks for a more substantial impact."

"Let's craft a well-defined proposal targeting corporate entities and their CSR committees, outlining our Trust's mission, objectives, and the specific project seeking financial support. Our focus projects for fundraising will be on financially supporting and empowering women entrepreneurs, secondly providing medical and educational grants, and conducting investment education awareness programs. It's crucial to clearly articulate the positive impact our initiative will have on the community or cause.

Beyond fundraising through these committees, we should plan to seek support from their employees, encouraging them to volunteer with us in organizing campaigns for insurance awareness. In this regard, we aim to collaborate with IRDAI, promoting their 'Insurance for All by 2047' agenda." I say as I remove a notepad from my drawer and began jotting down objectives and to-dos.

"Yes, we should also start creating online channels and leverage social media campaigns to connect with potential donors in addition to engaging with these corporates. Let us also explore partnerships with businesses who doesn't get applicability in CSR, other non-profits, or influential individuals who share an interest in supporting women's entrepreneurship, education, and healthcare. Collaborations can help expand your reach and access additional resources." Rekha ji suggested.

"Yes, and for our donors, let's execute a donor recognition program to express gratitude and acknowledge their contributions. We can consider featuring their names on our website, providing consistent updates, or even organizing special events to show our appreciation," I recommended.

"Laxmi, to qualify for CSR funding, we must ensure compliance with the legal criteria specified in the Companies Act. This involves establishing a track record in fields like education, healthcare, women's empowerment, or other stipulated areas. We should prepare the necessary documents, as per the Companies Act, 2013, since companies involved in CSR activities can contribute to trusts that align with the Act's provisions. Let's engage a compliance professional to guide us through the legal procedures," suggested Rekha ji.

"Alright, let's conclude and finalize this by next week," I mentioned. "Alright. By the way, you mentioned you wanted to discuss something during our call. What was it?" Rekha ji inquired.

"Yeah, I'm considering investing in a pre-revenue startup," I mentioned. Rekha ji responded, "Oh, so our finance diva is venturing into angel investing!"

"Absolutely, and now that you're a seasoned angel investor, I'm counting on your expert guidance to navigate this exciting roller coaster," I shared with Rekha ji.

Rekhaji's eyes widened over her steaming cup of chai. "Okay, tell me more," she urged, leaning forward in anticipation.

Annexure

HEALTH INSURANCE:

Health insurance is a financial arrangement that provides coverage for medical expenses incurred by individuals, offering a safety net against the potentially high costs of healthcare services. Health insurance policies vary in coverage, but they typically include benefits such as hospitalization, surgeries, doctor visits, prescription medications, preventive care, and other medical services.

For women, health insurance is particularly crucial due to various reasons related to their unique health needs and societal roles.

1. Comprehensive Healthcare Coverage:

a. Women often have specific healthcare needs that go beyond routine medical check-ups. Comprehensive health insurance ensures coverage for a wide range of services, including gynecological care, mammograms, Pap smears (v. important – for cervical cancer), and maternity care.

b. Regular check-ups and screenings are essential for early detection of conditions such as breast cancer, cervical cancer, and other reproductive health issues. Health insurance encourages women to prioritize preventive care without financial barriers.

2. Maternity and Pregnancy Coverage:

a. Health insurance plans with maternity coverage are crucial for women planning to start or expand their families. These plans cover expenses related to prenatal care, delivery, and postnatal care, providing financial support during a critical phase of a woman's life.

b. Access to quality maternity care ensures a healthy pregnancy and delivery, contributing to the well-being of both the mother and the child.

3. Reproductive Health Services:

a. Women's reproductive health encompasses a range of services, including contraception, family planning, and fertility treatments. Health insurance plans typically cover these services, promoting family planning and reproductive choices.

b. Coverage for fertility treatments, when needed, can alleviate the financial burden associated with assisted reproductive technologies, making them more accessible for women and couples.

4. Mental Health Coverage:

a. Mental health is an integral component of overall well-being. Many health insurance policies include coverage for mental health services, ensuring that women have access to counseling, therapy, and psychiatric care when needed.

b. Women may face unique mental health challenges, such as postpartum depression or stress related to societal expectations. Mental health coverage fosters a supportive environment for seeking professional help without financial constraints.

5. Chronic Condition Management:

a. Women are more prone to certain chronic conditions, such as autoimmune disorders, osteoporosis, and thyroid disorders. Health insurance provides the necessary coverage for ongoing management, medication, and specialist consultations associated with these conditions.

b. Adequate coverage for chronic conditions ensures that women can effectively manage their health and maintain a good quality of life.

6. Emergency and Hospitalization Coverage:

a. Accidents and unforeseen medical emergencies can happen at any time. Health insurance provides coverage for hospitalization, surgeries, and emergency medical interventions, offering financial protection during critical situations.

b. Quick access to medical care without the worry of steep expenses is especially crucial for women facing emergencies related to childbirth complications, accidents, or sudden illnesses.

7. Prescription Medication Coverage:

a. Women may require prescription medications for various health conditions, from chronic diseases to temporary illnesses. Health insurance plans often include coverage for a wide range of prescription drugs, making medications more affordable.

b. Affordable access to necessary medications ensures that women can adhere to prescribed treatments without compromising their health due to financial constraints.

8. Preventive Care and Wellness Programs:

a. Health insurance plans typically emphasize preventive care, encouraging regular check-ups, vaccinations, and screenings. For women, preventive care is essential for early detection and intervention in potential health issues.

b. Wellness programs included in health insurance plans may offer additional benefits, such as fitness incentives, nutritional counselling, and access to wellness resources.

In summary, health insurance is necessary for women as it provides comprehensive coverage for their unique health needs, supports preventive care, and ensures financial protection during various life stages. It empowers women to prioritize their health and well-being without the burden of high medical costs, contributing to a healthier and more resilient society.

LIFE INSURANCE:

Life insurance is a financial tool designed to provide a financial safety net for individuals and their families in the event of the policyholder's death. It offers a lump sum payment, known as the death benefit, to the beneficiaries named in the policy. Life insurance is crucial for women for various reasons, encompassing financial protection, legacy planning, and ensuring the well-being of dependents.

1. Financial Security for Dependents:

a. Women often play key roles in supporting their families, whether as breadwinners or caregivers. Life insurance ensures that in the unfortunate event of their demise, their dependents are financially secure.

b. For single mothers or women who contribute significantly to their families, life insurance acts as a crucial financial safety net, covering living expenses, educational costs, and other financial obligations.

2. Debt and Financial Obligations:

a. Women may have financial responsibilities, such as mortgages, personal loans, or educational debts. Life insurance helps prevent these obligations from becoming a burden on surviving family members.

b. Life insurance policies can be structured to cover outstanding debts, ensuring that the family's financial stability is not compromised in the face of unexpected challenges.

3. Providing for Children's Future:

a. Many women prioritize their children's well-being and education. Life insurance enables them to create a financial legacy for their children, covering educational expenses and providing a financial cushion for their future.

b. Policyholders can allocate a portion of the death benefit specifically for their children, ensuring that their aspirations are not hindered by financial constraints.

4. Ensuring Financial Independence:

a. Life insurance, when structured appropriately, provides financial independence for women, particularly those without a stable income. It becomes a means to secure their own financial future and that of their dependents.

b. Through policies under the Married Women's Property Act, women can secure life insurance benefits exclusively for themselves and their children, insulating them from external financial claims.

5. Legacy Planning and Estate Protection:

a. Life insurance is a vital component of estate planning, ensuring that women can leave a financial legacy for their heirs.

b. By naming beneficiaries and structuring policies wisely, women can protect their estates from potential estate taxes and legal complications, providing a smooth transition of assets to the next generation.

7. Business Protection for Women Entrepreneurs:

a. Women entrepreneurs and business owners can use life insurance to protect their businesses. Key person insurance or buy-sell agreements funded by life insurance can safeguard the business in the event of the owner's death.

b. Business debts, operational expenses, and succession plans can be addressed through strategic life insurance policies.

In summary, life insurance is a crucial financial tool for women, offering protection, financial security, and peace of mind. It empowers women to plan for their financial future, support their families, and leave a lasting legacy. Whether single, married, working professionals, or stay-at-home moms, women can tailor life insurance policies to align with their unique needs and aspirations, ensuring a resilient financial future for themselves and their loved ones.

MORTAGAGE LIFE INSURANCE:

Mortgage life insurance, also known as mortgage protection insurance, is a specialized form of life insurance designed to provide financial protection for homeowners and their families in the event of the policyholder's death. This insurance is specifically tied to a mortgage, aiming to ensure that the outstanding mortgage balance is paid off, preventing the risk of foreclosure and providing financial stability for surviving family members.

Consider the scenario of a married couple, Renuka Devi and her husband (if they had mortgage life insurance), who decide to purchase their dream home through a home loan. Both contributing to the household income, they recognize the importance of securing their investment and the financial responsibility tied to the mortgage. To protect their home and provide financial stability for the surviving spouse in the event of an unforeseen tragedy, she and her husband choose to invest in mortgage life insurance.

Tragically, her husband, the primary breadwinner, passes away unexpectedly. In this challenging time, the mortgage life insurance policy they had wisely purchased comes into play. The insurance provider is informed of her hudband's passing, and the policy's death benefit is processed.

The outcome is that the insurance company directly pays the death benefit to the mortgage lender, ensuring the complete settlement of the outstanding balance on the home loan. This means that Renuka, the surviving spouse, is relieved from the financial burden of the mortgage. The family home, filled with sentimental value and memories, remains in Renuka's possession, providing a stable living environment during an emotionally challenging period. With the mortgage settled, Renuka can focus on healing and making decisions about the future without immediate financial pressures. In this way, mortgage life insurance serves as a vital financial safety net, preserving the family home and offering peace of mind during a difficult time of loss.

In an alternate scenario where Renuka's husband, the primary breadwinner, did not have mortgage life insurance, the financial implications for the surviving spouse, Renuka, would be considerably different. Without the protective shield of mortgage life insurance, Renuka would likely face significant challenges in maintaining the family home and managing the outstanding mortgage.

In the absence of insurance coverage, husband's passing would leave Renuka solely responsible for the mortgage payments. The financial strain of managing the mortgage on a single income or unstable income could potentially lead to difficulties in keeping up with monthly payments. This situation might, unfortunately, result in the risk of foreclosure, putting the family home in jeopardy.

The absence of mortgage life insurance could intensify the financial burden on Renuka during an already emotionally challenging time. Without the insurance proceeds to settle the outstanding balance on the home loan, Renuka might be forced to consider alternative living arrangements or face the prospect of selling the family home to cover the mortgage.

Incase Renuka's husband had a general life insurance policy provides a lump sum payment (death benefit) to the named beneficiaries, the creditors, including the mortgage lender, may have the legal right to make claims on that money to settle outstanding debts, such as the remaining mortgage balance. Utilization of life insurance proceeds to settle outstanding debts, including a mortgage, depends on the specific terms and conditions outlined in the insurance policy and applicable laws.

This comparison underscores the critical role that mortgage life insurance plays in providing a financial safety net for surviving spouses. In its absence, the surviving partner may encounter formidable financial challenges and uncertainties, emphasizing the importance of proactive financial planning, especially when it comes to protecting assets like a family home.

LIFE INSURANCE under the Married Women's Property Act (MWP Act):

Life insurance under the Married Women's Property Act (MWP Act) is a legal provision that grants married women in jIndia the right to secure life insurance policies for their benefit and that of their children. Enacted in 1874, the MWP Act ensures financial autonomy for married women by allowing them to independently own and manage life insurance policies. These policies are structured to provide exclusive protection, shielding the insurance proceeds from potential claims by creditors or legal complications. The act empowers married women to make independent financial decisions, protecting the policy benefits for their well-being and that of their children. This legal framework offers a crucial avenue for married women to secure financial security and independence within the context of family and estate planning.

Claiming Insurance Policies

In the realm of financial literacy and independence, it is paramount for every woman to not only be aware of their own & spouse's insurance policies but also to actively engage in securing and understanding the policies. The significance of this knowledge extends beyond the realms of mere financial awareness; it is a crucial step towards ensuring financial security and overcoming potential hurdles that may arise in the future.

Why is it Essential?

In the event of a spouse's demise, knowing how to claim insurance benefits is vital for financial stability. Understanding the claims process ensures a smoother experience during a challenging time, helping women navigate complex paperwork and procedures.

Women need to be aware of potential hurdles in the claims process, such as incomplete documentation or delays.

Proactive learning and preparation can help avoid such pitfalls, ensuring a swift and efficient claims settlement.

How to Claim Insurance Policies:

1. Gather Documentation:

a. Collect all relevant documents, including the policy document, death certificate, and identification.

b. Ensure that the documentation is complete and in order before initiating the claims process.

2. Contact the Insurance Provider:

a. Notify the insurance company/agent promptly about the demise of the policyholder.

b. Seek guidance on the required documentation and procedures for filing a claim.

3. Beneficiary Information:

a. Clearly understand the beneficiary designation in the policy.

b. Provide accurate information to the insurance company to avoid any disputes during the claims process.

4. Understand Policy Terms:

a. Familiarize yourself with the terms and conditions of the policy.

b. Be aware of any specific requirements or exclusions that may impact the claims process during the time of the purchase of policy.

Consider a scenario where a woman, unaware of the specific documentation required for a life insurance claim, faces delays in processing the claim after her spouse's demise. The lack of understanding regarding the necessary paperwork, such as the submission of a valid death certificate or beneficiary details, can lead to extended waiting periods and additional stress during an already challenging time. In contrast, a woman well-versed in the claims process would proactively gather the required documents, expediting the claims settlement and ensuring financial stability for her and her family.

Knowledge is a powerful tool for financial empowerment. Every woman should actively engage in learning about their spouse's insurance policies and secure their own coverage. Understanding the intricacies of the claims process is crucial to overcoming potential hurdles and ensuring a smooth transition during difficult times. By actively participating in financial decisions and acquiring the necessary knowledge, women can safeguard their financial future and that of their families.

CHAPTER 10

SHARK TANK – MUMBAI STYLE

THE SHARKS ARE ALL ABOUT ROI,
NOT JUST A GOOD STORY.

I took a deep breath, the aroma of cardamom and ginger swirling around me. "So, for the past two days, I've been meeting this incredible young woman named Rhea Kapoor. Now, I won't bore you with the serendipitous details of how our paths crossed or the fascinating backstory of her startup, but let me tell you, I'm genuinely smitten with her vision."

A smile played on Rekhaji's lips. "Smitten, you say? That's quite the endorsement coming from you, Ms. Finance Diva"

I chuckled. "Well, the feeling's mutual, I assure you. Rhea's not just another entrepreneur with a half-baked idea. This girl has something special. She's building an e-commerce platform, unlike anything I've seen before. Imagine a virtual haven for fashionistas, a treasure trove of stylish apparel, but with a twist – every thread woven with a deep commitment to sustainability."

Rekhaji's eyebrows shot up. "Sustainable fashion? That's certainly intriguing. But is she, you know, ready for the big leagues? Running a business is no walk in the park, especially for someone young."

"True," I admitted. "Rhea might not have the seasoned experience of a seasoned tycoon, but her raw talent and passion are undeniable. And have you seen the app she's developed? It's sleek, intuitive, and so user-friendly, it practically begs you to shop guilt-free. I have a feeling this could be the next big thing, Rekhaji. A wildfire waiting to ignite the market."

I leaned closer, my voice laced with conviction. "That's why I'm considering investing. Not a small sum mind you, around 3 crores. I believe in Rhea, in her vision, and in the potential of this game-changing platform. It's a leap of faith, yes, but one I'm willing to take."

Rekhaji's gaze met mine, a flicker of admiration dancing in her eyes. "You've always been a woman who follows her instinct, Laxmi. And when it comes to spotting potential, you rarely miss the mark. This Rhea, she sounds like a force to be reckoned with. Now, let's see if your conviction is as contagious as you think. Investing based on a gut feeling? You're a brave!" Rekhaji chuckled, sipping her tea.

"And, by the way, given your seniority at the bank and the fact that a loan for Rhea's Adventure was previously rejected, I hope you are taking a formal approval from the bank before moving forward with this investment."

"Of course, I will apply for the approvals. But you're the angel investing guru! Tell me the good stuff – what do I do before I jump in?"

"First," Rekhaji winked, "be like Sherlock Holmes on steroids. Dig into the startup's numbers, their plan, everything! Don't trust pretty smiles, ask tough questions."

I scribbled on a napkin. "Got it. Due diligence like detective work."

"Exactly! Next, don't be shy about the price tag," Rekhaji grinned. "Remember, you're more than just money. Your advice, your connections, they're gold too. Negotiate fair, but don't be a Scrooge." My brows furrowed. "Negotiation – like a friendly haggle, not a war." "Precisely!" Rekhaji nodded. "And remember, investing is a long-term dance, not a quick salsa. Be patient, be supportive, but don't forget to hold them accountable. You're partners, not cheerleaders."

"Partnership – a marathon, not a sprint." I replied, grinning, a mix of nerves and excitement buzzing beneath my skin. She explains things so well—it's mind-blowing. I wish I had that knack for captivating storytelling.

"There you have it, Laxmi! Dos and don'ts for your angel investing roller coaster. Now, go grab those founders and turn your gut feeling into gold! Just remember, even with my advice, the ride might get bumpy. But embrace it, learn from it, and most importantly, have fun backing brilliant minds!"

"Now, before you waltz into your first startup boardroom," Rekhaji continued, "let's talk valuation. It's like deciding the price tag for a dream, a delicate dance between potential and reality."

I, all ears, lean forward. "That sounds… complicated."

"Nah, just common sense!" Rekhaji reassured me. "Imagine, you have this amazing app, brimming with possibilities. But what's it worth? Here's how we figure it out."

Look Back, Look Forward

"Think of it like buying a vintage car. We consider its past – how far it's driven, any bumps it's hit. Is it a rare model with shiny potential, or a common one needing a tune-up? Similarly, we look at the startup's progress – traction, revenue, customer base. The further they've gone, the higher the value."

Peek into the Future

"But a vintage car also has hidden potential – maybe it's the next collectible! So, we peek into the future. Industry experts, analysts, they play fortune teller, estimating how far this startup can fly – market size, competitive landscape, their unique edge. The brighter the future, the higher the price tag."

The Balancing Act

"Finally, it's not just about numbers, Laxmi. It's a negotiation, a balancing act. You, the investor, consider your risk appetite, how much you're willing to bet on this dream. The founders, they consider their future needs, how much fuel they need to keep flying. Ultimately, the price lands somewhere in the sweet spot where both sides feel excited, not squeezed."

"So, it's like appraising a treasure, looking at its history, its potential, and figuring out a fair price that makes everyone happy?" I reaffirmed.

Rekhaji chuckled. "Exactly! You're a natural, Laxmi. Now, there are fancy formulas and reports, but don't let them intimidate you. Remember, your gut feeling, combined with these basic principles, is a powerful tool. Go get that valuation done, see the startup through your investor lens, and trust your instincts. The most recommended course of action is to engage the services of a professional valuation firm. The world of angel investing awaits! Discounted Cash Flow (DCF) analysis will be more granular valuation method commonly used in angel investing, particularly for early-stage ventures where traditional metrics like revenue may not be fully established."

"But remember - Equity management, investor relations, and compliance seem like potential bottlenecks." Rekhaji said, "As your investments diversify, managing ownership structures, communication, and legal requirements can become incredibly time-consuming and error-prone. That's where a comprehensive equity management solution company comes in. It streamlines all aspects of equity management, from cap table maintenance and investor relations to comprehensive compliance support. Cap table maintenance.. That's always been a headache. Manually updating spreadsheets, tracking dilution... Their secure, cloud-based platform keeps your cap table accurate and accessible, automatically reflecting share issuances, transactions, and dilution calculations. Think real-time visibility and minimized risk of errors."

It also takes into account investor relations. Keeping everyone informed and engaged can be a challenge. The investor portal of such companies streamlines communication. Securely share documents, updates, and financial reports with investors, and facilitate Q&A sessions and voting processes. Picture improved transparency and enhanced investor confidence. It also acts as your compliance compass. Automated workflows and expert guidance ensure adherence to relevant regulations, minimizing legal risks and maximizing investor protection. You can sleep soundly knowing you're operating within the boundaries."

"Rekhaji," I began, her voice laced with a quiet yearning, "all this talk about Rhea's vision, building something impactful… it makes me question my own trajectory. Here I am, scaling the corporate ladder, wielding spreadsheets like a scepter, yet… is this enough? What about my 'never retire' dream?"

Rekhaji, seasoned in the art of deciphering unspoken desires, smiled knowingly. "Ah, young one, your ambition reaches beyond quarterly reports, doesn't it? You crave a legacy, a purpose etched in something more than balance sheets."

I nodded. "I can see a flicker of self-doubt flickering in your eyes, Laxmi" Rekha ji said. "Precisely! I admire Rhea's audacity, her passion for sustainability. But can I, a cold-blooded finance professional, ever tap into that kind of creative spark? And would angel investing, with its inherent risks, be the key to unlocking it?" I continued.

Rekhaji leaned forward, her voice dropping to a conspiratorial whisper. "Investing, Laxmi, isn't just about numbers. It's about backing stories, betting on potential. And what better story to invest in than your own? Angel investing can be the incubator for your 'never retire' dream. Think of it as your pre-retirement portfolio, not of stocks and bonds, but of experiences, relationships, and the thrill of knowing you nurtured innovation, empowered changemakers."

"You're saying... angel investing could be my bridge to a more purpose-driven life, even before I 'retire'?" I said.

Rekhaji chuckled, the sound as familiar and comforting as the chai. "Absolutely! Imagine mentoring Rhea, guiding her through the financial labyrinth. Imagine the satisfaction of seeing her vision blossom, knowing you played a part in it. That, my dear, is a dividend that no portfolio statement can match."

But the ever-cautious finance professional in me reared its head. "Investing in a startup is a leap of faith, Rekhaji. What about security? My retirement corpus? Can I afford to take such a risk with my hard-earned money?"

Rekhaji nodded, her gaze steady. "The path of the angel investor is rarely paved with roses, Laxmi. Due diligence is your shield, your sword. You must dissect Rhea's plan, scrutinize her numbers, understand the market forces at play. Remember, this isn't a gamble, it's a calculated bet. Come, let's sit in the veranda. The AC in your cabin doesn't suit me."

We head towards veranda. And so, the veranda transformed into a classroom, Rekhaji the professor, patiently unravelling the mysteries retirement planning.

"But beyond the numbers, Laxmi," Rekhaji emphasized, "remember the human element. Connect with Rhea, understand her vision, her team, her fire. This isn't just about ROI, it's about backing a soul you believe in, a purpose that resonates with your own."

As the conversation wove its way through the twilight, the veranda became a crucible of introspection.

"But wouldn't this mean juggling careers, managing risks, venturing into the unknown?" I asked, my voice a blend of apprehension and excitement.

"Rekhaji shook her head with a knowing smile, "Welcome to the 'never retire' club, Laxmi! Life, like Rhea's app, is an iterative process. There will be pivots, adjustments, even stumbles. Our ancient texts refer to Laxmi mata as "chanchala," (चंचल) emphasizing that Laxmi is always dynamic and ever-changing. Similarly, our lives, financial graphs and bank accounts exhibit the same unpredictable nature, sometimes soaring high and at other times facing downturns."

You spend all day talking to Rhea, and it's only a matter of time before those youthful whispers seep into your own thoughts. Soon, she'll be telling you about retiring at 40 to jet-set around the world. That's the trouble with these youngsters – their expectations float like wispy clouds, completely detached from reality."

And reality, she pointed out, has teeth. It bites in the form of underestimated costs. Travel and retirement, my friend, are not cheap adventures. One unexpected medical bill, one market dip, and suddenly those dreamy plans evaporate like morning mist.

Then there's the question of health. We can preach 'early retirement' all we want, but life, unfortunately, has its own script. Early retirement assumes a healthy, spritely 80-year-old you, gallivanting across continents. But what about unforeseen illnesses, accidents, or the creeping toll of time on our bodies? Medical expenses can devour an entire nest egg faster than you can say 'bucket list.'

And let's not forget the allure of a fulfilling career. Sure, youngsters today dream about sun-kissed beaches and exotic bazaars, but what about the satisfaction of building something, contributing to the world, leaving your mark? Early retirement might steal away years of potential growth, years of honing your skills and making a true impact.

But Rekhaji wasn't just looking back. She winked. 'Remember our generation? We worshipped silvered temples of wisdom, trusted salt-and-pepper hair to guide us at the boardroom tables. Now, we're the ones shaking our heads at the audacious dreams of the young. But maybe, just maybe, there's something to learn from both sides.'

'Perhaps,' Rekhaji concluded, tapping her armrest, 'the wisest retirement plan isn't a number on a calendar, but a heart and mind open to the endless possibilities that unfold before us, at any age, in any chapter.'

"Rekhaji, in my current role as a Chief Investment Officer (CIO), my focus is on managing portfolios for High Net Worth Individuals (HNIs) and Ultra High Net Worth Individuals (UHNIs). Typically, clients approach me around the ages of 35, 40, or 45, seeking guidance on retirement planning with the goal of retiring at 60, 65, or 70. As a CIO, I adopt a long-term approach, aligning a mutual fund's philosophy with my vision and ensuring that each fund manager's tactics contribute to the bigger picture.

Clients entrust me with substantial sums of money, and as an ideal CIO, I advise them to follow asset allocation principles. Based on their risk profile, I recommend investing a lump sum, inquire about their desired retirement corpus, and calculate the SIP (Systematic Investment Plan) amount for each month until retirement. Upon retirement, we discuss options such as SWP (Systematic Withdrawal Plan) to manage their accumulated corpus. However, if a 25-year-old approaches me with the desire to retire at 40, the situation differs. At this stage, individuals may not have a significant lump sum unless they possess generational wealth. Their SIP amounts might be relatively low, potentially leading to a disparity between their targeted retirement corpus and the realistic outcome. Addressing these challenges requires a different strategy, taking into account their early career stage and limited financial resources." I ask.

"You handle big money, Laxmi. HNIs, UHNIs, they come to you with piles of cash and dreams of fulfilling retirements. But yes - what about the Davids, the young ones just starting out, barely with a pot to piss in? They want to retire at 40, too, but with peanuts in their pockets! How do you, the master conductor, orchestrate their financial symphony?"

Rekhaji's smile widened. "Laxmi now you see the real dance! For these Davids, forget lump sums, we play a different tune. Small, steady SIPs are their steps, building their kingdom brick by brick. Their dreams might seem like moonwalks, but hey, let them dream! We guide them to realistic goals, maybe phased retirements, not all-or-nothing leaps."

"The key is time, their biggest weapon. We start them early, even with tiny SIPs. Time and compounding interest, that's their magic potion. Risk? We balance it like tightrope walkers, a bit of thrill but not enough to tumble. Lifelong learning is their safety net, new skills to open doors even after 'retirement.'

"Rekhaji," I said, a newfound seriousness creeping into her voice as she stirred her second chai, "the buzz of Rhea's success... it's intoxicating. But amidst the celebration, a thought keeps nagging at me and if she or this new generation plans early retirement – Inflation. A valid concern. The very dream of financial independence, the lifeblood of 'retire at 40' can be eroded by this insidious beast. The cost of living, our constant companion, can morph into a cunning thief, stealing away the value of our savings, our investments, our future".

"Rekhaji," I continued, my voice laced with a worry more pronounced than the Mumbai humidity, "I'm beginning to see the mirage in this early retirement plan. Early escape at forty, exploring the world, living free from spreadsheets… what if inflation just sucks the sand from under their dreams?"

"Concerns are valid. Forty seems like a distant oasis to them now, but the erosion in purchasing power due inflation can shift the landscape in ways we don't anticipate."

A shiver will run down their spine if they see how numbers are not co-operating. The image of her meticulously planned early retirement, built on spreadsheets and financial projections, suddenly will feel fragile, precariously balanced on the shifting sands of rising prices. The dream villa in Tuscany just will morph into a cramped studio at home."

Annexure 1 -
Chart Your Course to Financial Freedom

Plan	Risk Tolerance	Investment Type	Assumed Return	Monthly SIP	Total Corpus after 15 years	Withdrawal per month	Assumed Post Retirement Return	Total Withdrawal	Final Value after 25 years of Retirement
Conservative	Low	Debt-oriented Hybrid Funds, Fixed Income Instruments	9%	₹25,000	₹95,31,095	₹50,000	8%	₹1,50,00,000	₹2,20,91,588
Balanced	Moderate	Mix of Debt & Equity - Equity Oriented Hybrid Funds, Mid-Cap Equity Funds, Diversified Equity Funds	11%	₹25,000	₹1,14,71,439	₹50,000	8%	₹1,50,00,000	₹3,63,34,052
High-Risk	High	Predominantly Equity - Diversified Equity Funds, Low-Risk Equity Funds	13%	₹25,000	₹1,38,92,032	₹50,000	8%	₹1,50,00,000	₹5,41,01,630

Note: None of the calcualtions are inflation adjusted.

Annexure 2:

Discounted Cash Flow: Seeing is Believing (in the Future)

Imagine you have a magical money machine that spits out a certain amount of cash every year. How much would you be willing to pay for this machine today? This is the essence of Discounted Cash Flow (DCF), a financial analysis tool used to value investments by considering their future cash flows.

Why is the Future Important?

A rupee today is worth more than a rupee tomorrow. That fancy latte you're enjoying right now brings more joy than the one you'll buy next year. This concept, called the time value of money, is a core principle in DCF. DCF recognizes that cash flows received further in the future are less valuable than those received sooner.

How Does DCF Work?

Cash Flow Forecast: This is the foundation. You estimate the amount of cash the investment will generate in each future period. This could be profits from a business, rent from a property, or dividends from stocks.

Discount Rate: This is your magic ingredient. It reflects the time value of money and the riskiness of the investment. Higher risk demands a higher discount rate, making future cash flows less valuable today.

Discounting to Present Value: Here's the math part. Each future cash flow is discounted back to its present value using the discount rate. Imagine shrinking these future rupees to its current size.

Sum Up the Present Values: Add up the present values of all the future cash flows. This magic number represents the Net Present Value (NPV) of the investment.

So, What Does NPV Tell You?

Positive NPV: The investment is a winner! The future cash flows outweigh the initial investment.

Negative NPV: Oof, avoid this one. The present value of future cash flows is less than the initial investment.

DCF: Not a Crystal Ball, But a Powerful Tool

DCF is a powerful tool for appraising various investments, from stocks and bonds to real estate and business ventures. While it relies on forecasts, it helps make informed decisions by considering the time value of money and the element of risk.

DCF is a framework, and its accuracy depends on the accuracy of your cash flow forecasts and discount rate. But even with its limitations, DCF can be a valuable companion in your financial decision-making journey.

CHAPTER 11

DIAMONDS AIN'T FOREVER, BUT KNOWLEDGE IS

DIAMONDS MAY BE A GIRL'S BEST FRIEND,
BUT STREEDHAN IS HER SECRET WEAPON.
IT SWOOPS IN TO SAVE THE DAY,
FROM EMERGENCIES TO EPIC INVESTMENTS.
IT'S YOUR CHANCE TO INVEST IN YOURSELF
AND BUILD A FUTURE AS FINANCIALLY FIERCE
AS YOUR WEDDING LEHENGA!

Rekha ji was sitting with a quiet grace, leaning against the railing. The soft breeze was playing with the silver threads in her hair. I always admired her, a quiet giant, a steely lady whose rise from the ashes of devastation had whispered legends in the bank's corridors. A close working partnership blossomed five years ago, during her reign as head of the Private Equity Department at Samruddhi Bank, just before she embarked on new horizons. And today, I finally dared to ask her, " Rekha ji, there have been whispers circulating in the bank about a challenging past for you, including the early loss of your husband. I've always refrained from prying into personal matters; hence I've never asked before. However, may I do so now if you're comfortable? There might be some extra ordinary story behind your strength and resilience."

"Extraordinary? Perhaps, it was just life, lived one step at a time." Rekha ji, ever the pragmatist, said. She paused, and then began, her voice low and gentle. "I was barely twenty, a small-town girl married into a life of sunshine and laughter in Kutch. Then, just seven months into my pregnancy, the earth moved. The earthquake in Kutch, Gujarat… it swallowed our home whole, my husband with it. I woke up trapped, darkness pressing on my chest, the screams of the world muffled by dust and debris. Before I could even register the tremors as an earthquake, my home had already descended into the ground, trapping me and my husband inside. My husband lost his life on the spot. Panic fueled my limbs as I clawed my way out, desperate for a single breath. Back then, finances were largely a man's domain, especially in small towns. I, like many women, wasn't involved and had no clue about my husband's bank accounts. In the mess, I remembered my streedhan, a pouch with my gold jewellery tucked away in the damaged wardrobe. So, the gold jewelry gifted to me at my wedding wasn't just a sentimental keepsake; it was a lifeline. A tangible memory of a life lost, yet a symbol of my own will to survive.

I tucked potli safely against my waist. Barely twenty and heavy with child, I was then rescued by the rescuers. My world had shrunk to the barest essentials – my unborn child and the glimmer of gold hidden beneath torn fabric.

After that my brother brought me to his place in Bombay where I delivered my child. I found sanctuary at his home, not comfort. His own life a hand-to-mouth struggle, and I couldn't bear to be another burden. Yet, I had a daughter, Aanya, a tiny fist of life defying the cruel hand of fate. The gold, my streedhan, became my lifeline. It held the value of 5 lakhs from those bygone days. I traded it for a roof over their heads, for milk in Aanya's bottle, for textbooks under her tiny fingers. Nights were spent learning alongside Aanya, our cramped room lit by a single bulb. But my hunger for knowledge burning brighter than any hardship. A ray of hope arrived in the form of an NGO working for empowering women. They generously funded my college tuition, allowing me to enroll in a local college and embark on a new path with a degree in finance. To support myself further, I also worked part-time as a cook.

Days turned into years, each coin carefully budgeted, each sacrifice a silent hymn to Aanya's future. After I finished my graduation, I found work at a bank. Every promotion, every raise, was a brick laid in the foundation of Aanya's dreams."

"It's incredible to see you using your own experience to empower other women now, through this Sahyogini trust," I remarked, touched by her story. A gentle smile graced Rekhaji's lips. "Life teaches you a lot, doesn't it? It can break you, yes, but it can also show you incredible strength within yourself. Now, I get to use that strength to help others find theirs" she said.

The winds of change are sweeping through society, empowering women to claim their financial independence and chart their own destinies. In this journey, Streedhan, the age-old tradition of wealth bestowed upon a bride, transcends its cultural roots to become a potent tool for modern women seeking financial freedom. But how do we unlock its true potential and transform it from a cherished gift into a springboard for a brighter future?

Streedhan isn't just a collection of trinkets and heirlooms; it's a treasure chest overflowing with potential. Unlike the restrictive shackles of dowry, Streedhan is a symbol of empowerment, a celebration of your right to own your sparkle and shape your future. Imagine a vibrant tapestry woven with threads of independence, financial security, and the freedom to chase your dreams – that's the power Streedhan holds.

Think beyond the glitz and glamour of jewelry. Every gift, every asset you receive through life – from your doting grandparents to that thoughtful present from your college roommate – becomes your exclusive domain. It's a legal fortress, enshrined in the Hindu Succession Act, protecting your ownership even amidst life's storms. This isn't just about claiming your rightful inheritance; it's about claiming your agency, your right to be the architect of your financial destiny.

But Streedhan isn't merely a shield; it's a potent weapon in your arsenal. Need a war chest to weather life's unexpected blows? Streedhan can be your emergency fund, a safety net woven with threads of self-reliance. Dreaming of owning your corner office and calling the shots? Streedhan can be the seed capital for your entrepreneurial journey, fueling your ascent to financial independence.

The possibilities shimmer like the facets of a well-cut diamond. Upskill, pursue that coveted degree, or finally launch the business idea that ignites your passion – Streedhan can be your springboard to self-actualization. Diversify your portfolio, explore the world of stocks, bonds, or real estate, and watch your wealth blossom under your wise stewardship. Invest in a haven of your own, be it a cozy apartment, a sprawling farmhouse, or a rental property that generates passive income – the choice is yours.

Remember, the future isn't just about financial security; it's about creating a legacy that reflects your values. Use your Streedhan to empower others, support causes close to your heart, and leave a mark on the world that extends far beyond material wealth.

And you're not alone in this empowering journey. The government stands beside you, cheering you on. Tax benefits tailored for women investors are your allies, offering a helping hand as you climb the ladder of financial freedom.

So, embrace your Streedhan, not just as a possession, but as a symbol of your inherent strength and potential. With knowledge, strategic planning, and a dash of audacity, you can transform it into the key that unlocks a world of possibilities. Remember, the power has always been within you; Streedhan simply helps you unleash it, letting your true brilliance shine brighter than ever before.

Rekha's story paints a heartwarming picture – her Streedhan, a symbol of tradition and empowerment, paved the way for her daughter's initial education. However, this snapshot from the past doesn't fully capture the complex reality of financing education in modern India. Escalating costs, often reaching crores, have rendered Streedhan, while significant, often insufficient to solely bridge the gap. Education loans, once rarely considered, have become an increasingly common, yet concerning, solution.

Statistics paint a stark picture:

Education loan borrowers surged from 5 to 7 million: Between 2019 and 2023, the number of individuals seeking education loans in India witnessed a staggering 40% increase.

Loan amounts skyrocketed to Rs 17,668 crore: Disbursed education loans reached an alarming high in 2022-2023, reflecting the growing burden of educational expenses.

Outstanding loan portfolio ballooned by 17%: The amount of unpaid education loans reached a staggering Rs 96,847 crore, highlighting the widespread reliance on debt financing.

Even studying abroad paints a similar picture:

Students relying on loans nearly tripled: From 2012 to 2022, the number of students who used loans to study abroad almost tripled, soaring from 22,200 to a concerning 69,898.

Even prestigious institutions witness loan reliance: At institutions like IIMs, where education holds immense value, a staggering 85-90% of students rely on loans, highlighting the pervasive nature of cost barriers.

Needless to say, Education is a passport to opportunity, but the ticket can come with a hefty price tag. Enter the education loan, a powerful tool that unlocks doors, but also carries the weight of long-term debt. Before you or your children embark on this financial adventure, let's equip you with the knowledge to navigate it like a pro.

First things first: Is this loan your only key? Scholarships, grants, and even strategic part-time hustles can lighten your load. And hey, is the ROI worth it? Will your future earnings outshine the loan's shadow? Remember, sometimes a smarter path lies in online courses or local universities. Plus, living frugally now means less to borrow later – think ramen over restaurant nights!

Borrowing smart is key: Compare lenders like a knight comparing swords! Seek out government-backed options for their shining armor of low interest rates. Remember, borrow only for education, not that fancy gadget. Treat that loan like a focused beam of light, illuminating your studies, not your shopping sprees.

Repayment: Your financial warrior training: Start chipping away early, even while studying, to slay the interest dragon. Explore income-driven plans, flexible allies in your fight. And if opportunity knocks with lower interest rates, refinance your loan – that's like finding a magical potion for even faster debt slaying!

Beyond the numbers: Debt can be a mental monster, but you're not alone. Talk to your support squad, your family and friends, for encouragement and a shoulder to lean on. Don't shy away from professional financial advice – they're your wise mentors in this quest.

Remember, you're more than your debt: Take care of yourself! Financial stress can be a dark cloud, but self-care is your sunshine. Prioritize your mental well-being, for you are a shining star, and your journey shouldn't be dimmed by temporary burdens.

Imagine you're considering a one crore education loan to finance your studies. Here's a breakdown of how loan terms can impact your EMIs and total interest paid:

Tenure (Years)	Interest Rate (%)	Monthly EMI (Rs.)	Total Interest Paid (Rs.)	Total Amount Paid (Rs.)
5	9.5	₹2,10,019	₹26,01,111	₹1,26,01,111
10	9	₹1,26,676	₹52,01,075	₹1,52,01,076
15	8.5	₹98,474	₹77,25,305	₹1,77,25,305

As you can see, shorter loan tenures come with higher EMIs but lower total interest paid. Conversely, longer tenures result in lower EMIs but a higher overall interest burden. Taking out a one crore education loan is a significant decision, and navigating the repayment journey requires careful planning and strategic action.

Choosing the Right Loan:

With a higher income, a larger EMI becomes viable. Consider a manageable range of 40-50% of your salary.

Crafting Your Repayment Strategy:

Start early: Having a short tenure not only helps in reducing cost of the loan but also gives a peace of mind much earlier.

Embrace biweekly payments: Effectively making an extra payment per year, reduces the loan term and saves interest.

Exceed the minimum: As your income increases, consider increasing your EMI. Here's the impact on the 10-year loan:

₹1,50,000 EMI: Reduces loan term by 2 years & 3 months.

₹2,00,000 EMI: Reduces loan term by almost half, to only 5 years & 3 months.

Optimizing Your Loan:

Rate reduction: Securing a 1% interest rate reduction (8%) saves ₹6.42 lacs approximately over the 10-year tenure loan.

Moratorium magic: Utilizing a 6-month grace period for interest-only payments saves interest compared to full EMI payments during the grace period.

Create income: With a higher income through additional income streams it allows for significant prepayments, potentially saving years and money in interest.

Additional Tips:

Avoid capitalized interest: Making minimum payments during the grace period leads to less interest being added to your principal.

Consolidation/refinancing: If you have multiple loans with higher interest rates, consolidating or refinancing for a lower rate (e.g., 8%) could save you tens of thousands in interest.

Swap to a lower interest rate loan: Explore the possibility of converting your high-interest education loan to a lower interest rate loan, such as a home loan, through a process called loan balance transfer. This option requires owning a property or having someone close to you co-sign the loan. Remember, transferring the loan may come with processing fees and other charges, so carefully evaluate the overall benefit before proceeding.

These are just examples. Consider your specific financial situation, loan terms, and eligibility for loan transfer options before making any decisions. Seek professional advice if needed. With a higher income and effective strategies, you can significantly accelerate your loan repayment and achieve financial freedom faster!

Note: Calculations are based on standard loan repayment formulas and may vary depending on specific loan terms and rounding.

Additional notes:

Remember that these are estimations, and the actual loan terms and interest rates may vary depending on the lender and your specific circumstances.

Exploring government-backed loan schemes with potentially lower interest rates could further decrease the total amount paid back.

Consider seeking professional financial advice to create a personalized repayment plan based on your unique situation and goals.

Tax benefits on paid interest (up to ₹3.5L) maybe applicable.

As a new-age, financially stable couple, planning for the arrival of a child in the near future is both exciting and daunting. In today's world, where education costs are soaring at an alarming rate, it's imperative to prepare wisely and strategically for your child's future. With education inflation averaging around 12%, school and college fees are doubling approximately every six years, placing significant financial pressure on parents.

Consider this: in 2009, the fees for premier institutions like the Indian Institutes of Management (IIMs) stood at a modest 5 lakhs. By 2014, this figure had tripled to 15 lakhs, and today, it exceeds 20 lakhs. This steep rise underscores the critical need for a robust financial plan to ensure your child's educational aspirations are not hindered by financial constraints.

Enter the 3-in-1 child account – a comprehensive solution designed for parents who are proactive about securing their child's future. This innovative account seamlessly combines banking, demat, and trading facilities, providing a streamlined approach to saving and investing for your child's education and other significant life events.

Here's how it works:

Both parents can contribute a total of Rs. 13,000 monthly (Rs. 6,500 each) towards the child's future. This structured saving plan ensures a disciplined approach to building a substantial corpus over time, setting the foundation for your child's financial security.

The key to maximizing the potential of the 3-in-1 child account lies in smart investing. By investing the accumulated savings in NIFTY 50 through Nifty ETFs, and all mutual funds as per financial advice, parents can tap into the growth potential of India's equity market. Popular options such as NIFTY BeES, Nifty 50 ETF, and NIFTY ETF offer accessible avenues for long-term wealth creation.

Let's break down the numbers:

With an annual investment of Rs. 1.56 lakhs, the total investment over 18 years would amount to Rs. 28 lakhs.

However, it's essential to adopt a dynamic approach by increasing the investment amount by 10% annually. This incremental strategy can significantly boost the final corpus, potentially providing nearly Rs. 1.87 crore for your child's higher education, travel, or marriage expenses.

Considering the historical average returns of 12% for NIFTY50, the growth potential is substantial. By the age of 18, your child could have a fund of approximately Rs. 1.87 crore, ensuring they have the financial resources to pursue their dreams without constraints.

In conclusion, the 3-in-1 child account offers a holistic solution for parents seeking to safeguard their child's future. By combining disciplined savings with strategic investments, you can lay the groundwork for your child's success, providing them with the resources they need to thrive in an increasingly competitive world. Start planning today and embark on a journey towards financial security and peace of mind for your family.

CHAPTER 12

SURPRISE! YOUR HUSBAND'S A CROOK

INTRADAY WALTZ
UNDER THE DISCO BALL!

As the discussion with Rekha Ji continued, my phone suddenly rang, and I noticed it was Pranav calling. Excusing myself, I answered the call.

"Hey Pranav, what's up?" I greeted enthusiastically.

"Laxmi, I have some exciting news!" Pranav exclaimed.

"Tell me!" I urged.

"I was thinking we could throw a surprise party for you today, inviting our friends and close colleagues. It'll be a pre-celebration before our trip, surrounded by our loved ones."

My eyes widened in disbelief. "A surprise party? Today?NO!"

"Yes, I've arranged everything and it's a backyard party!," Pranav confirmed. "So get ready to be surprised, my love."

"But how did you manage to plan this without me knowing? "Honey, you're a genius!" I exclaim.

"The backyard party idea? Brilliant! The fairy lights, the bonfire, the stories... you've captured everything I love." I continue..

"Glad you approve, Mrs. Pranav Singhania," Pranav's voice echoes through the speaker. "Now, about the guest list... The old gang, some new faces, just the right mix. You must have some kind of sixth sense when it comes to party planning..there's one exceptional guest too."

My smile falters slightly. "An exception?"

"One colleague from themy office," he admits. "Someone you, uh, might not be particularly fond of…"

"Mr. Sharma?" I blurt out, already dreading the answer.

"Bingo!" Pranav confirms with a nervous chuckle.

I groan dramatically. Mr. Sharma, infamous for his outlandish boasts and self-aggrandizing stories, could turn a relaxing bonfire into a competitive bragging fest.

"Remember that hilarious moment at his wife's retirement party we attended couple of month's ago? Dude was basically claiming he's the reason for Independence Day. He said he was born in 1948 and the British scrambled out of India in 1947, terrified of his impending arrival! He said and I quote – 'The British saw my brilliance and knew their reign was over' !" Silence hangs for a moment, then we both erupt in laughter.

"Anyways, just a heads-up, honey! The guests will arrive in an hour, but I desperately need your expertise in picking out the perfect blazer for the party. Can you hurry home so we can tackle it together before everyone gets here? My fashion crisis awaits your rescue!"

"I'm on my way!" I said and with that, the call ends. I HATE PARTIES!

The backyard buzzed with the joyous chatter of arriving guests. Fairy lights twinkled against the twilight sky, casting a warm glow on the makeshift dance floor and the crackling bonfire. Laughter erupted from a group gathered around Pranav, who was regaling them with a story about my childhood escapades. Even from a distance, I could hear Mr. Sharma's booming voice in the mix, punctuated by exaggerated gestures.

"I tell you, Laxmi's first words weren't 'mama' or 'dada,'" he declared, his voice echoing across the gathering. "'Intraday trading!' she proclaimed, a tiny financial genius in the making!"

I winced, hiding a smile behind my hand. It was impossible to take Mr. Sharma seriously, yet his outlandish claims never failed to spark amusement. Just then, Pranav joined my side, a hint of worry creasing his brow.

"Honey, I have a confession," he whispered, pulling you closer. "Mr. Sharma brought his... 'business associate,' Mr. Kapoor."

My eyes widened. Mr. Kapoor was notorious for his competitive spirit and ruthless negotiating tactics. The last thing I wanted was a boardroom rivalry spilling over into the party.

"Don't worry," Pranav continued, squeezing my hand reassuringly. "I already warned him to keep the business talk to a minimum. Besides, you know how to handle these things."

He was right. I had years of experience navigating office politics, and Mr. Kapoor's bluster wouldn't intimidate me. Taking a deep breath, I steeled myself for the encounter.

As I approached the group, Mr. Kapoor turned, his eyes widening in surprise. "Mrs. Singhania! Fancy seeing you hosting such parties! Birthday cheers to you," he said, extending a hand with a practiced smile.

"The pleasure is all mine, Mr. Kapoor," I replied, returning his smile with equal poise. "Though I must admit, I wasn't expecting to see you at a social gathering."

"Mr. Sharma here convinced me to broaden my horizons," he chuckled, sending a pointed look at his colleague. "He assures me this is 'the party of the century.'"

I couldn't help but let out a playful scoff. "That might be a slight exaggeration, but we do know how to have a good time."

The conversation flowed surprisingly smoothly. I discovered Mr. Kapoor had a hidden passion for classic rock, leading to a lively debate about the merits of Led Zeppelin versus Pink Floyd. Mr. Sharma, ever the opportunist, tried to weasel his way into the discussion, claiming he once jammed with Jimmy Page himself (a blatant lie I easily countered with a witty anecdote about my own musical "talent").

As the night wore on, the music transitioned to Bollywood hits, and the dance floor became a vibrant scene of twirling sarees and joyous abandon. Pranav pulled me into a spirited rendition of हो चांदनी जब तक रात, देता है हर कोई साथ तुम मगर अंधेरो में ना छोड़ना मेरा हाथ हो... जब कोई बात बिगड़ जाये जब कोई मुश्किलि पड जाये तुम देना साथ मेरा, ओ हमनवा his infectious energy and slow dance with me drawing others to join in. Mr. Kapoor, surprisingly light on his feet, showed off some impressive moves on Sholay's hits Mehbooba Mehbooba, much to everyone's amusement. Even Mr. Sharma, after a few too many glasses of punch, loosened up and attempted (with comical results) to recreate Michael Jackson's moonwalk.

Just as I were about to grab another slice of cake (courtesy of Pranav's masterful baking skills), a commotion erupted near the bonfire. Mr. Sharma, his voice thick with mock outrage, was arguing with a guest I didn't recognize.

"I tell you," Mr. Sharma boomed with a glass on whiskey in his hand, gesturing wildly, "I was born and brought up in America. The stock market trembled at my birth! The Dow Jones dipped a hundred points the day I entered this world!"

The guest, a young woman with a sharp wit, simply raised an eyebrow. "And what, pray tell, was the date of your... market-altering arrival?" she inquired, her voice dripping with amusement.

Mr. Sharma puffed up his chest, oblivious to the laughter rippling through the crowd. "1947, of course! The British couldn't handle my brilliance and..."

Before he could finish his outlandish claim, the woman burst out laughing. "Sir, it might be best to avoid deep conversations with Mr. Sharma while you're sipping on that drink... You had us all in stitches with that story about the Dow Jones moving because of your birth!."

As the laughter around Mr. Sharma's deflated ego subsided, a hush fell over the crowd. Mr. Kapoor, seizing the opportunity, cleared his throat and addressed the gathering.

"Speaking of blunders," he said with a sly grin, "I see some potential mistakes waiting to happen here tonight, especially when it comes to intraday trading."

I have absolutely no idea why Mr. Sharma abruptly changed the subject like that, leaving everyone completely bewildered. Well, maybe he was just a tad bit tipsy!

Intrigued, I chimed in, "Oh really? Care to elaborate, Mr. Kapoor?"

A playful fire ignited in Mr. Kapoor's eyes. "Absolutely, Mrs. Singhania. Let's start with the classic rookie mistake - overtrading." He pointed playfully at a nervous-looking guest. "You there, sir, trying to chase every little price movement? Recipe for disaster!"

The guest stammered, "But-but the market's so volatile..."

I stepped in, a mischievous glint in her eyes. "Exactly! Like a fickle Bollywood heroine, it can turn on you in a heartbeat. Remember, patience is key."

"And discipline!" Kapoor countered, raising a finger. "No emotional decisions fueled by fear or greed! Stick to your stop-loss and take profit levels."

The debate unfolded, weaving through common pitfalls like ignoring risk management, succumbing to FOMO (fear of missing out), and neglecting technical analysis. Each point sparked lively discussions, with guests sharing their own experiences and near-misses.

Pranav walked in the conversation, usually calm and collected, his face visibly felt a familiar competitive itch

"Intuition? In the market?" Kapoor scoffed playfully. "Data and analysis, my dear Mrs. Singhania, data and analysis!" Once again, I'm clueless about why Sharma kept shooting glances my way and aiming all his words directly at me. It's like I accidentally stumbled into his one-man show without even realizing it!

As the debate heated up, Pranav's expression darkened with frustration as he glanced over.

"Mr. Sharma," I cut in, addressing him directly. "Why are you telling me all this? I'm well aware of intraday trading basics."

He looked at me, a strange smirk playing on his lips. "Then perhaps you could have taught something to your husband, Miss CIO," he drawled, his voice laced with accusation. "He lost the company's money and mine, invested in the company while squaring off the position, using company funds for personal trading without informing us... and now he's pitching foreign direct investments with all unclean and fraudulent books!"

The accusation hung heavy in the air, a bomb detonating in the midst of the lively party. Everyone turned to stare, shock and confusion etched on their faces.

I felt a surge of anger mixed with disbelief. "What are you talking about, Mr. Sharma?" i demanded, my voice tight.

"Pranav would never—" I couldn't say anything further as I saw Pranav standing there frozen, unable to defend himself. His eyes held a glint of unspoken approval. I felt a cold dread creep into her heart, my mind reeling with conflicting emotions. Trust battled with doubt, love with the possibility of betrayal.

...............to be continued.

Notes